Parade of the Dead

Parade of the Dead

A U.S. Army Physician's
Memoir of Imprisonment by
the Japanese, 1942–1945

by
JOHN R. BUMGARNER, M.D.

Illustrations by
Doris B. Hayes

McFarland & Company, Inc., Publishers
Jefferson, North Carolina, and London

ISBN 0-7864-0131-1

To my dear wife Evelyn,
whose patience and encouragement
enabled me to persevere long enough
to complete the writing of this book

Contents

Preface

For nearly half a century I have been reluctant to talk, much less write, about my experiences in World War II. It is only very recently that, at the urging of family and friends, I have been persuaded to chronicle my small part in those vast happenings. I believe that those who were involved in that immense conflict in an active way are often interested in the tale of another largely because of the ways in which that story relates to their own experience. I would say that my tale resembles those of other participants in many more ways than it differs from them. To paraphrase Horace, "With a change of name, the tale could almost be told of any other comrade in arms." But of course every individual's experience is unique, and I hope that the unique aspects of my own story bear the telling. After all, the final story of that global conflict will be made up by the assembly of facts collected from thousands of small players on that immense stage.

The following persons aided me in completing the manuscript for this book: Drs. Judy and George Cheatham, professors of English at Greensboro College; Ms. Karen Webb, transcriptionist; Rev. G. W. and Miriam Bumgarner, who did the indexing; and the libraries of the University of North Carolina at Greensboro and the city of Greensboro, North Carolina. My longtime friend Bishop Ernest A. Fitzgerald of the United Methodist Church, Winston-Salem, North Carolina, urged and inspired me to write this book, and I thank him for his kind encouragement.

I wish also to thank my dear sister Doris B. Hayes, who is responsible for the sketches that appear in this book.

CHAPTER 1

Prologue

Through the barbed wire fence and past the guard towers, we could see very little over the extensive plain. To the north was a Filipino farmer driving a two-wheel cart, pulled by carabao, through the rain, mist, and mud. Toward Manila, 65 miles to the south, Mt. Aryat and a few bamboo huts rose above the almost unrelieved flatness. It was the rainy season, a weary, dreary rainy season. The surroundings in and around the prisoner-of-war camp at Cabanatuan, the Philippines, were bleak at best, but during the rainy season the dreariness was unrelieved. Even when it was not raining, the sky was overcast. Every step we took was on sticky, wet, boggy ground.

That morning, like every morning, I left my bahay early to witness the parade of the dead, the burial procession of American prisoners of war who had died in the camp during the previous 24 hours. That morning there were 29 bodies. Sometimes there were

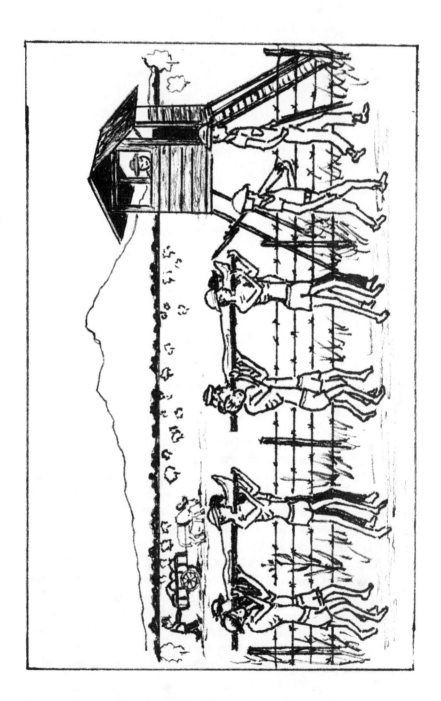

only 10 or 12, sometimes as many as 60 or 70; eventually over 2,500 prisoners of war died at Cabanatuan between April and December 1942. A few were killed by the Japanese guards; some died of battle wounds; but most succumbed to slow, debilitating diseases – malaria, dysentery, cholera, and general malnutrition.

The bodies were carried on litters improvised from bamboo shutters torn from the windows of the old Filipino army barracks which now served as our prison. The men of the graveyard detail were not in much better condition than their burdens. Both cadaverous, the borne differed from the bearers only in that they no longer breathed. Spectre-like and emaciated, the bearers grimly slogged through the sticky mud, some of them almost staggering under the burden.

At least the bearers did wear khaki shorts and wooden clogs; the dead wore nothing. Their few miserable possessions had been collected, then passed on to the living who needed the clothes. The emaciation of the dead was accentuated by their complete nakedness. Their ribs stood out from the thorax as if the skin, devoid of subcutaneous fat, had been drawn tightly over the ribs. Their eyes were sunken deeply into the sockets. The young lieutenant in charge of the burial detail always tried to close the mouths of the dead, but in many instances he could not because rigor mortis had set in. Mouths were partially opened and lips partly drawn back to display teeth in sardonic grins. Occasionally the grinning teeth clinched a dogtag, the only identification these men took to their common grave.

Ditches for the mass burials were dug on the day before by the grave detail. During the rainy season the graves were partially filled with water, which made it very difficult to cover the bodies decently.

I do not know exactly what drew me and the hundreds of prisoners to watch such a sad spectacle, but we lined the roadside each morning in a grim silence to watch, filled with both grief and hatred – grief for the dead, hatred for the enemy. The dead were sons, fathers, and husbands who in a different time had known love and the joy of living. Brought to the Philippines largely by sheer chance, as most of us were, the dead had fought bravely for over three months on starvation rations, all the while infected with malaria and afflicted with dysentery, before suffering the greatest defeat of any U.S. army in the field. Now, in this pit of misery called Cabanatuan, they were

Opposite: The parade of the dead, Cabanatuan POW Camp.

to be dumped summarily, without rites or observances, into a mass grave.

I suppose we, the living, came to some extent simply because we still could, because we were not yet dead ourselves. Beyond that, though, I know that we came to acknowledge and to affirm their and our own humanity. Regardless of their condition now, these miserable corpses had once been alive and had endured with us like men; we therefore owed it to them and to ourselves to bury them, to the extent we could, like men.

CHAPTER 2

From Medical School to the Military

May 1939–December 1940

When I graduated from the Medical College of Virginia, I was awarded, in addition to my M.D., a certificate reading "John R. Bumgarner, First Lieutenant, Medical Corps, Reserve, U.S. Army." This was the highest military rank, up to that time, which had ever been held by a member of my family. An ardent candidate for membership in the Daughters of the American Revolution, my Aunt Phoebe, while probing in the murky remote past, had once discovered that one of our direct forebears had achieved the great distinction of becoming a second lieutenant in the Home Guard during the American Revolution. The reserve commission awarded me and a number of my fellow graduates was, of course, a gift; and one should be wary of Greeks on such occasions.

Once recruited, we reservists-to-be had two encounters with the colonel who had done the recruiting, the first occurring during our perfunctory physical on the sixth floor of the clinic building at MCV. This was the first and last time that I ever viewed my modest classmates parading in the nude. Some of us were quite shy and much averse to such exposure without the benefit of even a towel. One of my classmates, John Stone, mentioned unkindly that I bore a remarkable structural resemblance to Mohandas Gandhi; another wanted to know when I had traded legs with a stork. As a result of long hours of study, lack of exercise, and too many calories, no one in our group could be considered a prime physical specimen. The examination was a farce and, I believed, would have discovered no physical shortcoming less obvious than a missing leg.

The next meeting was in a large classroom, where the candidates for a commission were assembled. The colonel met us there and delivered his induction spiel. "The army is expanding, and we need more medical officers in reserve," he explained, "but the chance of your being called to active duty is remote to nonexistent." After that persuasive discourse we decided – almost to a man – to sign up. After all, when we finished our residency and went into private practice, that Medical Corps certificate would look very patriotic and decorative on our office walls. On graduation night most of the males in the graduating class of '39 made two trips to the podium to receive certificates, one from the Medical College of Virginia, the other from the U.S. Army. There were a few male members of the class whose superior wisdom dictated that they not have such an intimate relationship with the army. My mother, a member of the graduation audience that night, told me afterwards that she had great misgivings about my having suddenly become part of the military establishment.

After graduation I returned home for a few weeks to play before starting my internship. During that interlude I loafed, occasionally looking in the mirror to address my reflection as "Doctor." Not once, though, did I salute myself as "Lieutenant Bumgarner." I had almsot forgotten my exalted military rank.

On the first of July 1939, I reported to Baroness Erlanger Hospital in Chattanooga, Tennessee. At that time the internship was rotating; we interns were on call two nights out of three, and we had little time for worrying about the outside world. I did read a newspaper occasionally, and I knew of the German threat in Europe. (The Germans would invade Poland two months later, of course, on September 1.) I was also aware that the Japanese had controlled Manchuria since 1931 and, after invading in 1936, controlled much of China. Yet somehow I felt that what was happening in these far-off lands could not possibly touch me in any way.

The fighting in Europe and Asia was not a prominent part of everyday conversation, and I saw few uniforms on the street. There were reminders, however, that we were at least indirectly involved. The railway yards were within two miles of the hospital, and night after night I looked out of my window to see the sky ablaze with hundreds of burning freight cars. When I asked, I was informed that the cars were being burned for scrap iron to send to Japan. I could not imagine, nor did I inquire, what that scrap iron was being used for.

Among the house staff at Erlanger, we talked about our hospital work and our plans for our nights off. Although most of us had reserve commissions, we did not mention war. The one journal I subscribed to, the *Journal of the American Medical Association* (on $25 per month I could afford no more), listed the names of the reserve officers being called to active duty. Around the new year 1940, I began to notice that more and more of the doctors I knew were included in that list. Still, I did not think I would ever be included; surely the army would let me finish my training.

In July 1940 I finished my rotating internship at Erlanger. At that time I was interested in pediatrics, so I began a residency in pediatrics at T. C. Thompson Children's Hospital there in Chattanooga. The work was interesting and I enjoyed it very much, but what then began to catch my attention was the fact that many of the medical school graduates of the class of '39 were getting the summons from Uncle Sam. Indeed, the names of many of my own classmates were appearing on that list. I finally decided that I must face what seemed inevitable; I left my residency and went home to North Wilkesboro, North Carolina, to practice with a friend of mine until I received the beckoning nod from the War Department. My friend, Dr. James McNeil, had a very active practice, and I was kept so busy that I soon forgot all about the conflict in Europe and Asia. I met a very pretty schoolteacher, and we started seeing each other quite frequently. Between my love life and the practice of medicine, world affairs were not prominent in my everyday thinking. The pretty schoolteacher, Evelyn, my wife for the last 46 years, says that I never at that time mentioned the possibility of marching off to war. My life continued thus, without a care, until early December 1940.

My parents lived about six miles out of North Wilkesboro, and I went quite often to visit them and to pick up my mail, which was being sent there. At least, I thought I had been picking up my mail. When I phoned on December 8, 1940, my dad, after some general conversation, remarked rather casually, "By the way, there's some mail here for you. There's one letter from the War Department, but you've been getting those letters off and on for a year, so I don't suppose it means anything." I visited Millers Creek early the next morning to look at my mail.

There was, indeed, a letter from the War Department:

By direction of the President and under authority contained in Public Resolution Number 96, by the 76th Congress, approved August 27, 1940, First Lieutenant, John Reed Bumgarner, Medical Reserve, 0-381108, First Military Area, Route #1, Box 43, Wilkesboro, North Carolina, is ordered to active duty for a period of one (1) year effective December 7, 1940. On that date he will proceed without delay from place shown after his name to Fort Knox, Kentucky, reporting after arrival to Commanding Officer for duty with the Fifth Medical Battalion. He will rank from December 7, 1940. If not sooner relieved, he will be relieved from active duty at the place where he is on duty in time to enable him to arrive at his home December 5, 1941. Procurement authority covering pay and allowances will be furnished by Commanding General, Fifth Corps Area. The travel is directed as necessary into military service, FD 1324, P15-0621, 1378, 0700, 0284, 0730, A1505-01, and 2. A copy of voucher covering payment of travel or value of transportation furnished, and cost of packing, crating, and shipment or value of transportation requested furnished and cost of packing, crating, shipment of authorized baggage in compliance with this order will be furnished, Commanding General, Fourth Corps Area.

By command of Brigadier General Smith J. N. Thompson, Colonel, GSC Acting Chief of Staff.

OFFICIAL C. A. MITCHELL,
Colonel AGD Adjutant General

Those orders, although impressive, were beyond my understanding. I should have known the notice was coming, but I must say that I was really surprised. I had been so busy and so interested in my work and in Evelyn that I had forgotten how vulnerable I was. It amazes me now that both my parents and I were so cavalier about my probable induction.

My mother and father saw the surprise on my face and asked what was wrong. I told them, as well as I could, that I had been called to active duty but that they should not be alarmed; it was only for one year. I read the order a little more carefully, taking notice of the date I was due at Fort Knox. I then looked at the calendar; it was December 8. I was already one day late. I wondered just what view the army would take of such dereliction and decided then, very suddenly, that I could not allow my offense to grow. I chatted with my parents for a few more moments and then returned to town. Making hurried trips to the office and to my room at the boarding house, I packed everything I owned into one suitcase, then went by the house where Evelyn was living. It was not yet 9 A.M. when she came to the door, and she was very surprised to see me. "What are you doing here so early on Sunday morning, especially without calling?" she asked. I explained the situation as well as I could. I believe that she was more shocked than I. We had been to a party the night before and I hadn't mentioned leaving town. We said goodbye. I assured her of what I had assured my parents: I would be home for Christmas in about three weeks. We were all to learn more about the ways of the military.

As I drove through our little hamlet, Millers Creek, I saw one of my old boyhood friends standing by the road. He told me five years later that he couldn't understand why I was doing all of that waving. He, Lawson Eller, was the last familiar person that I would see for over five years.

I took off over the mountains toward Fort Knox, spending that first night in Middlesboro, Kentucky. The next morning I started early, taking the route through Pineville and Corbin. As I passed through Pineville I drove over a long narrow bridge covered with ice. I slowed down and was proceeding with caution, but in the rearview mirror I saw a big new Auburn approaching from the rear without slowing down. Perhaps the driver had not seen the ice. When he began to brake, his car skidded and plowed right into the rear of mine. My car went out of control and skidded into the side of the bridge; my front fender and bumper were so bent that both dug into the tire. A minute or two after we came to a standstill, a uniformed Pineville policeman drove up, siren going. This pompous lad got out of his car, looked at my North Carolina license, and, without speaking to me, addressed the driver of the offending car: "Mr. Land, would you like this man [meaning me] held for anything?" But before the native son could speak, another man walked up and announced that he had seen the entire episode, that the gentleman driving the big Auburn had caused the accident. He handed me his card; I noted that he was an attorney. The Pineville cop backed off, and the driver of the Auburn told me to take my car to a nearby garage where he would pay for the repairs. I somehow drove my car to the garage, and in a few hours I was on my way again with enough repairs to make my car roadworthy. That day, with my car still not steering properly, I drove to Bardstown. Already three days late and certain the military police were out looking for me, I spent a sleepless night in a Bardstown hotel.

I limped into Fort Knox the next day with my car veering drunkenly because of a front wheel that was still much out of line. I had some trouble finding the Fifth Medical Battalion, and when I did I was almost sorry. I walked into the grimy old temporary headquarters and, asking to see the commanding officer, was led to a potbellied stove in the middle of a large room full of officers who did not seem to be doing anything productive or even organized. Sitting next to the stove was a slender, gray-haired man who wore medical insignia and the eagles of a full colonel. I introduced myself, but the colonel didn't move. "Where in the living hell have you been, Lieutenant?" he barked. Abashed, I sputtered and tried to explain, but he waved me off: "Well, you're here, and in the Fifth Medical Battalion. You won't be treating sick patients. Your patients will be sick trucks." Since I didn't know a carburetor from a generator, this was not good news.

The colonel then ordered Captain James Vetter to show me to my quarters, a tent for two heated by a Sibley stove resting in the middle of a dirt floor. The Sibley stove had been in the American army for a long time, and it served poorly to heat a tent; quite frequently as much smoke came into the tent as went out the pipe, and every article of clothing, hung randomly around the tent, became grimy and sooty. The stove pipe in my tent, insecurely suspended by wires, was as inefficient as any. The soot seemed to stick to our skin and become ingrained. It was wintertime at Fort Knox, and that Sibley stove did little to keep us warm. Fortunately the army issued enough blankets so that we didn't freeze after we went to bed.

One evening I attended a movie with my tentmate, another lieutenant. Returning to our tent, we childishly threw a few snowballs at each other. One snowball thrown very hard at me somehow missed its mark, striking the stove pipe above the top of our neighbor's tent dead center. Those officers, engaged in a serious game of poker, boiled out of that tent like a bunch of irate hornets. Tent pegs flew out from everywhere as they came out sputtering, coughing, and swearing. I was disillusioned that officers and gentlemen could use such language. Since we were the only persons in sight, they vented their tempers on us as we protested our innocence. "It was an accident," we repeated to an unconvinced audience. Things and persons finally settled down, and we inspected the damage: the pipe had been jarred loose from the stove and pounds of soot had been distributed evenly over the officers and their possessions. Only when I had retired to the safety of my own tent did I dare laugh.

My tentmate was a doctor from Georgia who, like myself, had been summarily uprooted. He was married and had three children, a lucrative practice, and a large mortgage. He did not believe he could support his family and pay his mortgage with a first lieutenant's income. His solace, like mine, lay in Uncle Sam's promise to send us home in a year.

The colonel was right that we weren't there to treat anyone for their ills. Just what we *were* there for no one seemed to know. Fort Knox and the Fifth Medical Battalion were trying to assimilate throngs of officers and enlisted men who were totally ignorant of the military. Here were all these men gathered together with no assignments, nothing to do. After breakfast each morning we reported to headquarters, and after that we were on our own. We attended no classes, received no instruction, performed no drills. Anything we raw recruits learned about the military seemed purely accidental. Since I was doing so little, it was hard for me to understand why the colonel had been so upset by my three-day tardiness.

I walked around for several days in civilian clothes until a regular army captain, apparently appointed to steer me around, took me to be fitted for my uniforms. I was so impressed with my appearance in the dress uniform that I almost immediately had myself photographed. I liked the pictures so much that after sending one to Evelyn, I distributed several copies to my relatives. I felt that my soldierly appearance would reassure those who felt our country was in peril. I earned my pay modeling my new uniform and watching the bulletin board.

Rumor was that our quarters at Fort Knox were temporary and that we would be moving soon – where, we did not know. Apparently the business of training and indoctrination was to come later. The regular officers seemed pleasant and competent, but too much raw material had arrived for them to assimilate on such short notice. Finally a notice appeared on the bulletin board: On or about December 15, the Fifth Medical Battalion was moving to Camp Custer.

Only the competence of a few regular officers and old-time sergeants enabled us to get ready to leave for Camp Custer. We were finally given a date for departure, and since I had very few possessions, planning was not difficult. Actually the enlisted men prepared us for departure. All of the tents had to be taken down on the day we left and turned in to the quartermaster. The night before departure the officers with their luggage were quartered in a very large warehouse-like room where we slept, or tried to sleep, on the floor. The next morning wakeup was at 6:00 A.M. We ate breakfast at the usual mess hall and reported to the army trucks to make the journey to Camp Custer. For our noon meal en route we were issued three sandwiches: ham, jam, and peanut butter. We threw our luggage into the back of the truck and waited while all of the vehicles were assembled. By 8:00 A.M. we were told that the trucks would have to pass in line before a reviewing stand so that the commanding general could salute us and signal our departure. At 9:30 he and his staff finally appeared; we were allowed to pass slowly in front of the reviewing stand while the solemn and sacred ritual of a limp salute was performed by the commanding general.

Finally we were on our way to Camp Custer. Fort Benjamin Harrison was to be our halfway point, and we made it there in spite of a large number of trucks dropping out for repairs. I never learned whether the fault lay in the machines themselves or in the young mechanics who repaired them. Apparently these young recruits had not yet become fully competent in ministering to ailing trucks. We left Fort Benjamin Harrison the next morning after bed and board and headed for Camp Custer, where we arrived before dark. Two enlisted men had driven my '39 model Ford coupe all the way since for some unrevealed reason the officers were not allowed to drive their cars on this trip. I was happy to find that my car had had a safe trip. The enlisted men were happy for the chance to drive instead of riding in an army truck, though they, like the rest, were required to stay in convoy.

CHAPTER 3

The Route to the Philippines

December 1940–February 1941

We arrived at Fort Custer 12 days before Christmas, greeted by several inches of snow and ice. The battalion moved into what appeared to be brand new and previously unoccupied barracks, the ground around which was still littered with pieces of building materials. Apparently the Fifth Medical Battalion had been waiting for the carpenters to finish their job. These new barracks at least had indoor showers and toilets; at Fort Knox we had had to walk through snow and rain for at least 300 yards to a large facility which served scores of officers for bathing and other purposes. There were some pluses at Camp Custer, but the thing that remained the same was the tedium of our days. We seemed to be waiting for something to happen before we could get started doing something, I knew not what. During my entire time as a guest of Uncle Sam, I had not yet received one order to do one single thing.

A few days after arrival, I assembled with the other new reserve officers for a physical. I think that from the nature of that physical, which included no lab work or X-rays, only a catastrophic illness would have attracted the doctors' attention. The problem lay in the fact that there were too many new arrivals to do an adequate physical on everyone. I was weighed, and my bulk in shorts came to 128 pounds. After the physical I was told that, except for being 20 pounds underweight, I was a superb specimen. However, the military doctors presented a waiver for me to sign covering my lean state. When I asked what would happen if I didn't sign the waiver, the reply was that either way I would still be in the army. The army had a great desire to keep up with its paperwork, and I got the message that Uncle Sam would prefer that I cooperate in keeping the records straight.

One event out of the ordinary occurred soon after we arrived at Battle Creek and Camp Custer. The colonel issued an order that all officers were to assemble in the early morning for a five-mile hike. We did assemble and were led by a regular army staff sergeant. I think the sergeant took smug satisfaction in what he did to us, a bunch of soft civilian dentists and doctors, aged 28 to 40, who in general ranged from slightly overweight to downright paunchy. The fast pace quickly had us gasping for breath. One rather obese captain, a surgeon from Georgia, walked just on my right, struggling to keep up and panting for every breath. From his words I could tell that he resented the whole show. I heard him say between gasps, "What's that bastard trying to do, kill us?" Finally we began to drop out and limp home. I was able to stay the distance—largely, I think, because I wasn't carrying that waivered 20 pounds. While I was with the Fifth Medical Battalion, no one ever again mentioned hikes. We never understood the object of such a caper, which seemed to serve no purpose other than convincing us that the sergeant was a rare sadist.

Except for that brief break in the humdrum, nothing worth mentioning happened until the 17th of December. On that morning the adjutant announced that the colonel wished to call an officers' meeting in the headquarters building soon after breakfast, the first officers' meeting since our arrival at Camp Custer. Surely this meeting was an omen of something momentous.

Since there were no chairs, we all stood in a large circle once we were all present. After the adjutant called us to order, the colonel began to speak: "I want a volunteer to go to the Philippines. He must be a first lieutenant; he must be a medical officer; he must be single; and he must be a reserve." I heard him clearly; I scanned the gathered circle carefully and noted that I was the only person who answered that description. Sick of the cold boredom of Camp Custer, I held up my hand. The colonel looked relieved. I think he preferred that I volunteer rather than for him to conscript me. The next bit of news was that I was to depart for San Francisco on New Year's Day 1941. I had promised my family and my girlfriend to be home for Christmas. I would need to sell my car and solve several other problems before January 1. I had been so much involved with my profession that I hadn't looked, except for road maps, at any map for some time. I thought the Philippine Islands were only a few hundred miles off the coast of California and had forgotten that Manila was more than a third of the way around the world from North Wilkesboro. Anyway, I learned my geography lesson too late.

I got only half of what I had paid for my car four months earlier. I was able to get all of my possessions in one large suitcase. The battalion adjutant arranged for my train reservations, and I was off and away. I chose a day coach to save money, and, on January 1, I began my four-day train ride across the continent. Never having learned to sleep sitting up, I rested but little on my way to San Francisco. When I reported at the Presidio de Monte Rey, the port of embarkation, I was informed that there was some problem with our transport, the A. T. *Grant,* and that we would not be able to go aboard for four days. I, along with a new acquaintance, Second Lieutenant, Infantry Reserve, Jay Ryan, took a room in a cheap hotel near the Presidio. Jay and I began an acquaintance which I would treasure. He was a short, red-faced Irishman who was enthusiastic about everything and everybody. Jay had a little box camera with which he photographed everything in sight. I still have a great number of his snapshots. We killed our time while waiting for the departure of the *Grant* writing letters and going to movies. One picture we saw was *The Philadelphia Story,* the big box office draw at that time.

One letter I wrote at the hotel was directed to the Chief Surgeon, Philippine Department, U.S. Armed Forces in the Far East. "Dear Sir," I began. Having no training in army protocol, I wrote the letter in the same manner that I would if I were writing to my brother. I explained that I had not completed my postgraduate training and thus wished to be assigned to Sternberg General Hospital in Manila. Since I was noted for my terrible handwriting, I was extremely careful to make this letter capable of being deciphered. I walked about a mile and a half to a post office and sent the message airmail. Several weeks after I had arrived in the Philippines, I accidentally ran into the adjutant from the office of the department surgeon. He introduced himself, and after I told him my name and rank, he laughed. "Oh, you're that one," he said. "When I opened that letter of yours and handed it to the colonel to read, he turned livid – I thought he was going to have a stroke, but after a while he calmed down and started laughing. 'Let him have it,' he said. 'No one ever before in my experience had that much unmitigated gall.'" The adjutant explained that I could never fully realize how near I came to being sent to Mindanao (a rural Philippine posting, much less desirable than Manila). And so it was that I was assigned to Sternberg General Hospital.

Finally, after four days in San Francisco, we got the word that we were to board the *Grant* by 10:00 A.M. the morning of January 10. Jay and I were prompt in boarding. I must say that Jay's eagerness to be about Uncle Sam's business far exceeded mine. Jay, every ounce of him, yearned to become regular army. He was a reserve officer who had a brother-in-law in the regular army, and I believe this brother-in-law in Texas was his alter ego. Jay was very friendly to me, as he was to everyone, but he never ceased to try to correct my unmilitary manner.

The U.S.A.T. *Grant* seemed a huge boat to my eye, though in truth it was really very small. Quarters for the first and second lieutenants were far from elegant. Six of us – two doctors, two dentists, and two medical administrative corps persons – occupied that small space they called a stateroom. Four of us were first lieutenants, and two were second lieutenants. On each side of the 8' × 8' cabin was a triple-decker bed. All of our luggage had to be stowed in a corner or under the bed. When I walked into the cabin, the two medical administrative corpsmen, both second lieutenants, were stretched out on the lower bunks. I should have pulled rank then and there, but I was totally unversed in military protocol. I made the voyage on the top bunk, and I was to travel over 7,000 miles on that lofty perch. My cabin mates were amiable, and there was never a word said about anyone's preference in bunks. I thought my living quarters were rather cramped and shabby until I went below decks to visit the enlisted men's quarters; I also found out that the nearer one's quarters were to the keel the more apt he was to become seasick.

Just about the time the *Grant* left the bay, I developed a faint trace of unease which never left me while I was aboard. The transport was small; the ocean was big, always in motion, with a rise, a fall, and a sideslip – a gentle rise, a faster fall, and a lateral swing motion. At times when the motion was rough, the queasy sensation was much worse. Luckily, I never lost my food. I was told not to be sorry for myself since the troops in the hold were, in general, much worse off.

The dining room on the *Grant* provided food which would have been a credit to any fine restaurant; it was wonderful to behold, but the undulations of that little ship robbed me of any craving for that display of food. There would be times, several months later, when I dreamed about the wonderful fare aboard the *Grant*. In the mess I was seated at a table with other junior officers, none of whom had been afflicted with mal de mer, and one of the most unsettling things was the torture of watching those officers devour their food with such evident gusto. My newfound friend Jay Ryan was one of those who shared the table. He didn't help my predicament one iota with his almost ravenous appetite and his frequent questions about my malaise.

Transporting thousands of troops and thousands of dependents halfway around the world under the shadow of a known enemy seemed a routine matter, I suppose because the administration in Washington wished to believe, or perhaps wished everyone else to believe, that we were isolated from the rest of the world. There were some regular army officers on the *Grant,* but the majority were, like myself, green material. There were also hundreds of dependents, wives and children. There were several military wives on board who were obviously going to have babies born, either on the *Grant* or in the Philippines. I wondered at that time if a baby born on board would be eligible later to run for the presidency. The military and their dependents laughed, partied, and behaved as if they were on a lark; there was no mention of the shadow which loomed over the Pacific and no portent of the coming storm. When we crossed the International Dateline, everyone celebrated as if we were on a peacetime cruise. There was absolutely no indication that the same government which transported all those civilians thousands of miles away from

Denis B. Hayes

home would three months later send the *Washington* to carry them the 8,000 miles back to the United States.

The lounge or recreation room of the *Grant* was the site of bridge games interrupted only by meals and sleep; some played bridge all their waking hours from San Francisco to Manila. There was one high ranking officer's wife who seemed rooted to her seat, assured the choice spot by her husband's rank. Her partners, by her election, were the wives of other high ranking officers, but she outranked them. The pecking order in that room was questioned by no one. These ladies were so continuously occupied with the cards that they had time for little else. There were retainers on the boat, civilian employees who were involved in services to the passengers. Among the retainers was one elderly gentleman who had served as a civilian steward on the *Grant* for many years. His responsibility lay entirely in attending to the wants of those lofty in rank. He hovered around the lounge serving drinks, snacks, and whatever else the officers and ladies wanted. On one occasion he approached the table where the ladies of the more elevated rank were seated, and addressed one of them: "Mrs. Smith [not her real name], your bath is drawn." She tried to wave him off: "I don't want a bath now." But the retainer was insistent: "But Mrs. Smith, you haven't bathed in a week." Mrs. Smith, redfaced, flurried, and angry, made a hasty departure.

My friend Jay, during the daylight hours, continued to roam the deck to peek, peer, and snap his camera. Jay wanted to document completely his career as an army officer.

When the *Grant* arrived at Honolulu near the end of January 1941, we were met with all the fanfare accompanying arrival in the islands. We were supposed to stay in Honolulu for only one day, but fortunately the engines on the boat had to be shut down for repairs. We were told that the *Grant* would sail again in about five days, and we were privileged to eat and sleep on the boat while we toured the islands. I was delighted that as soon as the boat docked, my seasickness ceased, not to reappear until five days later when we were again at sea.

Honolulu was teeming with military personnel – about every second person I saw in Honolulu was in a navy, army, or marine uniform. The newspapers we saw were full of news about two men, Admiral

Opposite: The U.S.A.T. Grant.

Husband Kimel and Admiral James O. Richardson. *The Honolulu Advertiser* carried large pictures of both in their navy dress uniforms. There was to be a change in the Commander-in-Chief of the United States Fleet (CINCUS). The changing of the naval chief was attended with pomp that would occur but once in the career of any naval man. Of course, none of the military personnel from the *Grant* were invited, but the newspapers had full and elaborate coverage. Large pictures in the *Advertiser* showed the quarter deck of the battleship *Pennsylvania* weighed down with naval brass. There were presumed to be ten flag officers on that deck, and the remaining space was taken by naval captains and staff officers. It was a festival day for both the incoming and outgoing CINCUS. Thankfully, Admiral Husband Kimel was unaware of just how ill-fated this day would prove for him.

There were many beautiful things to buy in Honolulu, but I had neither money to buy, nor a place to store, any possible purchase. Our time in Honolulu was all too brief, and on the fourth day in harbor the bulletin board announced that the *Grant* would depart promptly at sunrise next morning. Not strangely, as soon as we left the smooth harbor and the *Grant* was subject to the undulations of the Pacific, my motion sickness returned.

We were at sea for about eight days before arriving at Guam and dropping anchor some distance from the dock. The water was much too shallow for a boat of any size to dock. Guam was not yet, in any way, prepared to participate in a Pacific war. Approaching the dock later aboard a lighter, I saw an unusual sight. Most of the crew had gone ashore earlier, and as we approached the docks we saw scores of the enlisted men lined up in front of what happened to be a row of small rooms. I was very curious to know what was happening, and I asked a regular army medical officer on board the lighter if the men were shopping for souvenirs. He thought my question was extremely funny. He said, "Oh yes, they are shopping and some will come away with a souvenir which will require weeks and a lot of sulfanilamide to treat." Then he explained, "If you must know, that is a brothel serviced by natives." There were no officers in those lines; any who were involved in such activity sought solace in a more private setting.

With an area of only 256 square miles, Guam, the southernmost island of the Marianas, lies a little over 5,000 miles west of the Golden

Gate. Its natives are of Chamorro stock with a strong mixture of oriental and occidental blood. We were told before we left the *Grant* that we were to be back at the dock in five hours to reboard our ship. Guam's chief significance at that time was as a relay station for the Pacific Telegraph Cable. Agana, the capital of Guam, was the only place we visited, and at that time it in no way resembled a tourist attraction, though there were scores of natives wandering around trying to sell trinkets of local craft. There were 75 marines, a few navy personnel, and a very small but well equipped naval hospital. I could not determine exactly what the 75 marines were doing on the island; indications were that they were there as a token representation with practically nothing to do. It was impossible to visualize how that tiny island in the backwash of the Pacific would later accommodate thousands of troops, five large airfields, and two deep water harbors.

The only exciting moment I experienced on the isle of Guam happened on my way down the hill from the hospital, when a very large iguana scurried across my path. The lizard was at least three feet long and seemed to be after me, although I was assured that the many iguanas on the island were perfectly harmless.

The next leg of our journey, Guam to Manila, was 1,500 miles, a five- to six-day journey. The passage was more of the same except for encounters with some of the characters on board the *Grant*. On the first day out of Guam the bulletin board showed lists of assignments to the different posts in the Philippines. There had been numerous listings for outfits on Corregidor and at Fort Stotsenburg, Clark Field, Fort McKinley, and others, but none for Sternberg General Hospital. I was beginning to feel like the forgotten man, when on the second day out of Guam the listing for Sternberg was posted and my name was on it. I was elated to see that my letter had been received and my request honored.

The most attractive part of the voyage came when we entered the San Bernardino Straits. From the moment we came into that passage between islands, the travel was as smooth as if we were on a pond, and my unease departed. With so much beautiful weather, a calm sea, and a tropical breeze, I chose a spot on deck near the bow. Sometimes the passage between the islands was so narrow I could see the beautiful scenery on either side.

During the passage, which took many hours, I became involved in conversation with two unusual characters. The first was a smooth-spoken young officer who wore second lieutenant's bars on his shoulders. He was about 25 years of age, rather handsome, and well groomed. The conversation was largely about the young lieutenant. I made no effort to elicit information from him, since there was never a need; it flowed freely from him. He told me that he was an MIT graduate in engineering; that the rank he wore on his shoulders was not his true rank (his actual rank, which for some reason had to be kept secret, was that of a major); that he was in military intelligence, which also had to be kept secret; and additionally, that he was assigned to the coding and decoding section of the military intelligence in the Philippine Department where his job entailed the interpretation of secret messages as they would come into the code room. I wondered greatly at the time what manner of man this was. He was in the secret intelligence, yet he kept no secret. A few months later I came in contact with an officer who was assigned to military intelligence at the Philippine headquarters, and I was very curious to know what had become of the young officer. I gave the gentleman from intelligence his name and description. The officer readily replied, "Yes, I know the officer; and his job involves little more than that of a file clerk." According to my informant, the young man in question definitely did not have clearance to the code room, and the rank of major was pure fiction. Baron Munchausen could have taken lessons from the young lieutenant.

Soon after the young lieutenant unloaded his classified secrets on a perfect stranger, another unusual character took his place. This officer, a captain in the quartermaster corps, was also anxious to tell his story. He had signed on for an indefinite stay in the army. I was curious why he, a man of at least 45, had signed up for a period of at least three years. His answer was that he wanted a change. I asked him why his wife hadn't come with him. He answered that his wife, a teacher, didn't want to leave her job. I asked him if this wouldn't mean that he would be away from her for at least three years, and he answered, "Oh, that doesn't matter. We have an understanding about such things." Since I was a bachelor and understood the marital state but poorly, I asked him more questions about the possible effect this would have on his marriage. "Oh, it's of no consequence; she left me alone once and spent two years in Paris studying and teaching languages." He added that in the past he had gone to South America alone to work for four years as a mining engineer. When I inquired about the possible effect that such a separation would have on his marriage, he answered, "Oh, none, when we are back together we resume our relationship as if we had only been away for a day."

CHAPTER 4

Manila

February 1941

We reached Luzon, the largest and northernmost of the Philippine Islands, and docked at Manila Harbor on February 20, 1941. All of those aboard, military personnel and dependents alike, were met by someone. Strangely, family members had come to be with various officers or soldiers already in the Philippines, though in May 1941, just two short months later, all of the dependents would be loaded onto the *Washington* for a return trip home. What did the State Department learn in May that it hadn't known in January? But that day we did not know how short the families' stay would be.

Although under U.S. control since the American victory over the Spanish in 1898, the Philippines were never an American colony. Neither were they, in 1941, quite a sovereign state, although they had been granted provisional independence by the U.S. Congress in 1934. The United States had extended a protectorate over the islands, backed up by 16,000 American combat troops on the islands under the command of General Douglas MacArthur, who also commanded the 12,000-man Philippine Scouts Division, the only combat-ready Philippine force.

I was met at the boat by Lieutenant Ernest W. Bye, Medical Administrative Corps, regular army, a fine and efficient officer. (Bye was killed January 9, 1945, when the *Enoura Maru* was bombed, and was buried in a mass grave at Takoa, Formosa.) He introduced himself, then startled me with his preliminary remark: "Don't get settled in too much, the Japs will be in here in three months." This sort of greeting just after I had set foot on Philippine soil was not calculated to be reassuring. Aside from those words of welcome, Lieutenant Bye was of great help. He was my billeting officer, and I had been assigned to the Luneta Hotel for living quarters. The hotel was very old, and hardly luxurious by American standards. There was a bath on every floor which at times was taxed to serve several men at once. Fortunately, all the occupants of the Luneta were men, so we did not have to stand on cermony as we entered and left the bath. My floor, the seventh, had a bath with four showers, five basins, and five commodes.

The Luneta Hotel was run by an old "sunshiner" (the name given to American servicemen who retired to the Philippines). When I inquired about his reason for being in the Philippines, he told me that he was wanted by the police back home in Tennessee. He had earlier been in the Philippines with the army and had liked it so well that when he got into trouble he came back with no intention of returning to the United States. I did not pursue that line of questioning any further. The sunshiner did run a good hotel, and the food was marvelous. Where else would one be served fresh mango or papaya on ice as a breakfast opener? I am sure, though, that the hotel made all its profits from the little bar in the narrow hallway leading to the dining room.

I didn't require much time to unpack. Most of my possessions were in one small footlocker – some clothes, three or four medical books, a stethoscope, a blood pressure instrument, and Evelyn's picture.

To my great surprise, my roommate walked in – the short, red-faced, red-haired, very military Jay Ryan. We had shared a hotel room in San Francisco for four days, had been good friends on the *Grant*, and here, by sheer chance, we were to be roommates. I wish someone would figure the odds against such happenings.

I was to report to Sternberg General Hospital the next morning, so I spent an hour or two walking with Jay around the Luneta, a large park across the street for which the hotel was named. Beyond the park we could see the plush gray luxury of the palatial Manila Hotel, where MacArthur and his wife and son occupied the entire top floor penthouse built as a gift for the general by Philippine President Manuel Quezon. To the east from the Luneta Hotel it was only three or four blocks to the Manila Bay and Dewey Boulevard. Jay, as I found out on that walk, was a stickler for military punctilio; on that walk, and all others thereafter, he insisted that I, due to my exalted rank, should walk on his right. I protested that rank among lieutenants was like virtue among courtesans. My arguments were of no use – I walked on the right.

After dinner on that first night Jay and I walked out on our small balcony which overlooked Luneta Park and Manila Bay. In the distance, across the bay to the east, we could see a big red full moon which was then within a few moments of setting over the Mariveles Mountains on the peninsula of Bataan. This startlingly beautiful sight was ours for the looking every evening at sundown. Before arriving in the Philippines I had never heard the word Bataan, and as I viewed that sunset – the rays coming in from the South China Sea and setting beyond the mountains – I had no hint of how well acquainted I would soon become with that malaria-infested jungle.

Having never traveled farther from home than Richmond, Virginia, I found much of interest in Manila. The hospital was only a few blocks east of the Pasig River, and after working hours I very frequently walked over the bridge, where in a few minutes I could be in the heart of downtown Manila, popularly called "the Pearl of the Orient." Bustling night and day, the city always seemed to be full of calasas (two-wheeled, open, horse-drawn vehicles) driven with such fury that it seemed there were a thousand Jehus holding the reins. There was always the clop-clop of the feet of the hundreds of little horses which drew the vehicles. Exceeding even the madness of the calasa drivers were the natives behind the wheels of the little taxi cabs. Those cabs were very tiny indeed; two people attempting to fit into the rear seat experienced real togetherness. Riding in that rear seat was always a white knuckle event. I never saw a traffic policeman while I was in the Orient, and the cab drivers wove crazily in and out of traffic with a total disregard for both fore and aft. The cabbies seemed to feel that if something bad happened it was fate.

Pervading all of downtown Manila was the odor of horse dung and copra. I must confess that I came to enjoy the odor. There was one truly modern store in the downtown area, the Botica Boie, which was stocked with American goods, but there were scores of little hole in the wall shops. I liked especially to visit the little bookshops where one could occasionally find some rare or unusual books, all sold at a very low price. I was particularly attracted to the doctors' offices which carried the unusual spectacle of neon signs in front. Through the 1970s the doctor in America who advertised was a social leper among his colleagues, but in the Philippines such blatant advertising, if not practiced by all, was far from rare. Many offices boldly displayed the doctor's name, place of training, and type of practice on multicolored neon signs: Dr. Luis Ramirez, Specialist in Women's and Venereal Diseases, Trained at Harvard. These signs never recounted fully, though, just how long the doctor had spent at Harvard or whatever other prestigious place was in question.

Surprisingly, the number of places one could go for amusement was very small. Many of the military personnel were regular fans of jai alai and bet heavily on their favorite players. Many went nightly to the Army-Navy Club where the amusement and the food were good. I didn't go often because my bankroll was so limited. I was sending the greater portion of my army monthly check to pay what was owed on my education. The Army-Navy Club was a haven for married couples who went to eat, dance, play cards, and watch the entertainment.

Since there were few single Caucasian females in Manila other than the nurses at Sternberg, some of the bachelor officers sought solace with the native girls, though such practice was not approved. Among my colleagues at Sternberg, Lieutenants Jack Comstock, Lloyd Goad, and Lester Fox were bachelors who regularly dated three attractive, well-educated Filipino girls. Two of them had been educated in prestigious schools in the United States.

In their ignorance my friends took those young ladies to the Army-Navy Club. They entered and were seated, all at one table. Some time went by, and all they got were glacial stares from those in attendance. More time passed, and still no waiter came near them. All of the army and navy men at the surrounding tables, with their wives and girlfriends, were given water and menus, and finally were served. Eventually, one of the young ladies at the neglected table politely observed that perhaps they should go elsewhere, which they did. Jack told me, when I inquired about their night on the town, that at first he felt what had happened at the club was just an oversight. However, he told me later that each one of the young lieutenants had two days afterward received in his mail slot at his place of work a note to the effect that natives were not welcome at the Army-Navy Club. I had always been led to believe that our colonial policy was paternalistic, even indulgent, and that we in no way had adopted the snobbery of British imperialism. To have been subjected to such exclusion must have been a great humiliation to the three women.

On July 1, 1941, the army decided to convert the Luneta Hotel into a noncommissioned officers' club. This meant that Jay and I would have to find new quarters. Three of my Sternberg colleagues invited me to share quarters with them: lieutenants Nelson Kaufmann, Julian T. Saldivar, and Ralph Hibbs. The quarters were nice and not too far from our place of work. We had (and I have not lived in such luxury since) a houseboy, a maid, and a cook. We paid the three of them a total of 75 pesos a month – about $37.50 American. In addition we gave each a ganta of rice each month. This seemed very little, but the wages for service had been set by some mutual understanding among the American military. To have exceeded those figures would have caused us to be frowned upon. Dominidor, the houseboy, ran the household, supervised the other house help, purchased all the food, and planned the menus. We knew, and there was a general understanding among the military, that the houseboy had an arrangement with his providers through which he was able to supplement his income. We were happy with the way things were, and to have mentioned the subject would have greatly upset the relationship. We knew, and Dominidor knew that we knew, but that was a line one did not cross. As long as the custom wasn't mentioned, it was the same as if it never existed.

When ladies were invited in for dinner, Dominidor stayed late to supervise the cook and to serve the meal. He did this with as much stately dignity as one would find at the Waldorf. Hibbs and Kaufmann were the gallants who most often brought young ladies to visit and dine. One of the young ladies was the daughter of a high-ranking general in the Philippine Army, and the other was the daughter of a Philippine senator. Both had been educated at prestigious women's colleges in the United States. The conversation when those young ladies were present was as good as the food. There was, however, one problem on those otherwise delightful occasions. Lieutenant Saldivar, "Poncho" we called him, had a wife and several kids back in Texas. He was overweight, jolly, and quite a lot of fun when with male company, but he took great delight in upsetting the polite company which came to our quarters to dine. He would wait until all except himself were seated, then make his appearance wearing nothing above the beltline. His manners were impeccable except, of course, for his attire and one other habit: he would wait till the meal was nearly over and then, to show his appreciation for the meal, belch loudly. Throughout the meals, the young ladies never let it be known by word or facial expression that there was anything unusual in Poncho's action or appearance.

Since the other American military installations – such as Corregidor, Fort Stotsenburg, and Clark Field – were some miles from Manila, we found that almost overnight we had developed a great number of friends who wanted any kind of shelter over the weekend. Our overnight friends didn't mind at all sleeping on the floor and accepting potluck at our meals.

Most of the military in the Philippines were behaving as if there were no war in Europe or a few hundred miles away in China. In fact, our first intimation that Washington had any concern about possible U.S. involvement came in May 1941, when thousands of dependents were sent home. There were a few officers who had a great desire to board the transport and go home to the States with their wives and children, and I could sympathize with them. The only way one could go home was by the way of a chronic severe illness. For example, the lieutenant colonel in charge of the lab at Sternberg developed a bleeding ulcer, and for that reason was sent home.

In September or early October 1941 one lieutenant was able to be sent home through such a device. He was admitted to Sternberg General Hospital with "vertigo." The neurologist examined the young officer and could find absolutely no sign of any organic disease. Major Steven Sitter, the examining officer, surmised that the young lieutenant must have read the book on vertigo, because he was able to

demonstrate every sign of the syndrome. It became very embarrass-
ing after several days to watch the young officer stagger all over the
hospital grounds. He made sure that he was seen by everyone as he
reeled around the compound. Finally his presence around the hospital
became so disturbing that he was sent home to be studied more in
depth. Interestingly, a lieutenant colonel stationed at Sternberg was
called home as well and arrived in Honolulu at the same time as the
vertiginous lieutenant. Writing back to Major Sitter, the lieutenant
colonel told of a stroll he took in downtown Honolulu. He noticed a
very familiar figure and profile just ahead of him on the boulevard –
the young lieutenant, walking with a powerful, resolute, non-verti-
ginous stride. The lieutenant colonel did not hail the young man, nor
did he see him later. He was amazed that a sea voyage could cure such
a severe case of vertigo.

My good friend Jay Ryan stayed in touch after we were evicted
from the Luneta Hotel. He was assigned to the 31st Infantry, which
had been going on frequent maneuvers in northern Luzon. Jay always
took his camera with him when he was out in the field, and he never
missed a target or opportunity to use it. He even made a couple of
trips to Sternberg, and while there photographed the entire hospital.
On maneuvers he left his unit as often as he could to visit the Igōrots,
a tribe of primitive natives living in the mountainous areas of northern Luzon. Jay made scores of pictures of these Negritos (Pacific
pygmies), who were originally a very warlike tribe but had become
less belligerent under first Spanish and then American occupation of
the islands. One large group of the Igorots living at the higher alti-
tudes in the mountains was responsible for the construction of very
extensive stair-like rice terraces. When one looks at the Igorots, it
seems almost impossible to imagine their having the engineering skill
to build those structures which would rival the pyramids in difficulty.
Jay also made dozens of pictures of the Flagaellantes, a religious cult
which is also found in northern Luzon. Probably their religion was introduced by the Spaniards. This religious practice was present in
Spain as late as 1820. Jay's pictures show the practitioners of this
ritual drawing blood from each other with leather thongs as a form
of penance. Jay wished, I believe, that at the end of an illustrious
military career he would be able to retrace his life in the military with
snapshots.

CHAPTER 5

Sternberg General Hospital in Peacetime

February 1941–December 1941

On February 21, 1941, I arose early for breakfast. This was to be my first day at Sternberg, so I wished to be ready. I left the hotel and walked the five or six blocks west down Gral Luna Boulevard toward the Pasig River. Gral Luna Boulevard provided a delightful walk, lined on either side with palm, plane, acacia, and flame trees. The trees, especially the flame trees, helped to start my day in an upbeat way. When I walked through the gate on that first day, Sternberg seemed very impressive. The facility was a group of two-story buildings connected by walkways at each level. The buildings forming the sides of a quadrangle all faced inward. Inside the quadrangle the

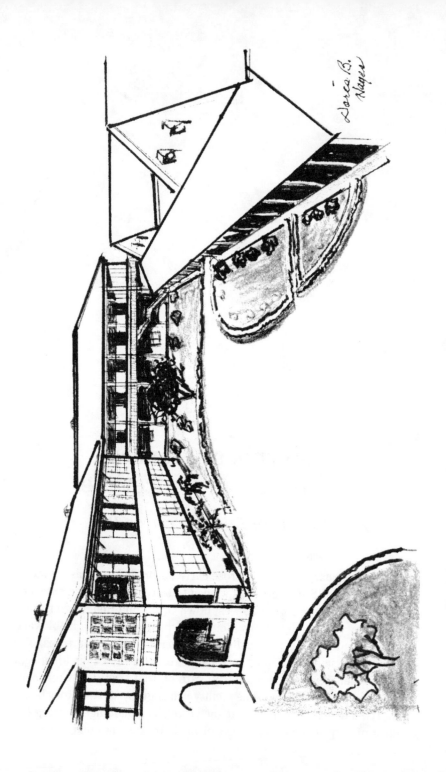

grounds were beautifully landscaped and planted with exotic native plants. The walkways were lined with trees. The whole area was tended by Filipinos who kept all the plants and trees very carefully manicured.

A young corporal led me to an inner office, where I saw a full colonel and a lieutenant seated at separate desks. The lieutenant got up immediately, and I saw that he was the same officer, Ernest Bye, who had taken me from the *Grant* to the Luneta Hotel. Lieutenant Bye introduced me to my new commanding officer. "Oh, you're the one," the colonel grinned. "I read your letter of introduction, and I wondered what you would look like." After the introduction, Lieutenant Bye, the adjutant of the hospital, took me to the office of the chief of medicine, Major James O. Gillespie, a no-nonsense officer who told me that I would be working on three different wards. He took me around the hospital and introduced me to the doctors, nurses, and corpsmen assigned to the medical service. I began to settle in at Sternberg, where I would remain till Christmas Eve 1941.

The hospital was a fortunate assignment for me. First, Major Gillespie was a very well-trained internist, who made frequent ward rounds and held weekly conferences. In addition, as one of the few peacetime Army general hospitals, Sternberg served a variety of patients. American army personnel, Philippine Scouts and dependents, and retired veterans were admitted to the hospital. Even so, Sternberg General Hospital was small — never more than 300 patients — since many patients were handled by station hospitals at such outlying garrisons as Fort McKinley, Fort Stotsenburg, and Corregidor.

I was assigned to work on three different wards: the BVA ward (Bureau of Veterans Administration), which cared for retired Philippine Scouts and old "sunshiners"; the tuberculosis ward, filled with both American and Filipino servicemen; and the dependents' ward, made up largely of children of Filipino Scouts. The latter was actually a pediatric ward. The BVA ward held about 60 patients in a large open ward. The senior ward surgeon was Captain Eugene Jacobs, regular army. Captain Jacobs was deadly serious about his work, and he was a very good doctor.

The patients on every ward were quiet, orderly, pleasant individuals, who cooperated fully in every way. The patients were largely

Opposite: Sternberg General Hospital, Manila.

admitted with medical problems, and the list of illnesses was not very long. Ninety percent of the admissions were due to malaria, dysentery, dengue, sprue, yaws, and all possible combinations of intestinal parasites, including amoebic dysentery.

Work on the ward was enlivened by the patients' many interesting stories. Some of the sunshiners had served in the Spanish-American War and remembered such famous men as the first Douglas MacArthur (Civil War general and first military governor of the Philippines, father of the more famous general); Emelio Aguinaldo, the famous Philippine insurrectionary leader; and William Howard Taft, who at one time served as High Commissioner of the Philippines. It was interesting to hear some of the Philippine Scouts and sunshiners tell about fighting the bolo-wielding Moros in Mindanao (the second largest of the Philippine islands). All of the events which these old soldiers related seemed to me as remote as the plains of Troy, but that war was as fresh on their minds as World War II is now on my own.

One particular sunshiner, James Hackett, caught my special attention. Well past 70 in age, he had retired in the Philippines because he loved the islands and the people, especially a Filipino girl. He returned to Sternberg General Hospital periodically for a checkup of some of his various disabilities. He related that he was a farmer who grew rice, bananas, mangoes, and papayas. I found that he owned one nipa hut, two water buffaloes, and innumerable ducks and chickens. I learned further that he had one wife and eight children. To extend the conversation with this very interesting gentleman, I asked him how long he had been married. "Married?" he retorted. "Married, that is the surest way to spile a woman." I learned that between sunshiners and native women a common law relationship was not unusual. Hackett was quite good at his second language, Tagalog. In this language he conversed very freely with some of the retired Philippine Scouts. I was quite curious about his skill at speaking Tagalog. Many career officers stayed in the islands for many years and never acquired a speaking knowledge of the native dialect. The enlisted men were the linguists. I finally asked Hacket how it had been that he had become so proficient in the language of his adopted homeland, when the officers had not learned a word of it. He replied immediately, "I had a long-haired dictionary."

I spent only two to three hours per day on the BVA ward. My work there was largely concerned with doing histories and physicals on admissions and writing orders for lab and medications. On the BVA ward we mostly treated endemic illnesses which were bound to recur — primarily malaria, because of the ever present malaria carrying mosquito.

There were also, in that retired group, many cases of sprue. This illness could better have been called a syndrome, and its etiology was, and is, very vaguely defined. It has been variously attributed to nutritional deficiency, infections, and toxins. The disease was characterized by loss of appetite, diarrhea, weight loss, anemia, and a distended abdomen. One could almost make the diagnosis by inspection when the patients entered the ward. They were pale, skinny, and had bloated bellies. Our treatment was largely iron and lots of brewer's yeast. Some of the Philippine Scouts had chronic malaria which never seemed to be adequately treated. Their numerous intestinal parasites and amoebic dysentery were treated with various vermifuges and emetine.

I spent three to four hours a day on what we referred to as a dependents' ward (the aforementioned pediatric ward used by the children of Philippine Scouts). Those children were in general a well-behaved group, and their fathers and mothers were always grateful to the doctor for his efforts. The children suffered to a great degree from the same illness as their parents, and my practice on that ward mainly concerned itself with malaria, dysentery, dengue, and intestinal parasites. Some of the children had severe anemia due to hookworm infection. Ninety percent of their ailments we were able to treat adequately.

Every hour of the day, there were visitors on the dependents' ward. If a child was very ill, the mother was allowed to sit with the child, bathe it, and feed it. The Filipino mothers seemed to be very caring and attentive. Some of the mothers of very ill children were permitted to spend the night.

We did have certain rules regarding visitors, though. No one was supposed to bring in food to the sick, but the enforcement of the rule was not very strict. One reason for the rule was the frequent introduction of certain objectionable items to the ward. A prime offender was the "balut," a fertilized duck fetus, still in the shell, developed to the point just prior to feathering. To the American palate, the balut was unsightly and unsavory. Even worse, after a few days without refrigeration, the balut issued an offensive odor – and it was customary, for at least some of the natives, to allow this delicacy to reach almost the end point of ripeness. In spite of the rule, it would have been highly offensive to this very sensitive people to be searched for such contraband. Those who worked on the ward waited patiently till all the visitors were gone, then made a search and got rid of the illicit item. No visitor ever inquired after the confiscated goods, so face was saved by everyone.

The visitors to the dependents' ward were attracted to some easily removable articles which rightfully belonged to the U.S. Army – towels, knives, forks, spoons, and even dishes. Here, too, there was the never-intruded area of understanding. We knew that small amounts of such items were regularly disappearing, but it was much better, it seemed, to lose a towel or spoon here and there than to humiliate one of these sensitive, delightful people. I recall one event very vividly. One very well dressed lady, the mother of an ill child, came into the ward to feed and bathe her beautiful little girl. The mother was wearing a transparent lace blouse. After feeding her child, she visited the bathroom and stayed an unusual period of time. When she came out of the bathroom and paraded toward the exit, I could plainly see displayed across her front and through the blouse, in bold red letters, "U.S. Army Medical Corps." I never once thought of arresting her progress toward the door.

The tuberculosis ward was small with no more than 20 patients. The beds on that ward were mostly occupied by Philippine Scouts who had developed the disease while in service. It was customary that as soon as the diagnosis was established, the patient was given a disability discharge and transported to one of the Philippine-run institutions. Having visited San Lazaro, the hospital for lepers in Manila, and the native-run tuberculosis hospitals, I very much hated to discharge those poor fellows because their prospects were not good under any circumstances. In all of the native hospitals the wards were so crowded that the patients in adjacent beds could easily reach out and touch each other. In each type of hospital it was possible to give little more than custodial care. Effective drugs for these diseases were not yet discovered. There was some collapse therapy done for tuberculosis patients: pneumothorax, thoracoplasty, and even lobectomies; but the resistance of the natives to tuberculosis was very low, and the prognosis was generally poor. Manuel Quezon, the president of the Philippines, had the benefit of the best treatment, both in the United States and Manila, but even he finally died of the disease. Quezon was so conscious of tuberculosis as a health problem in the Philippines that he built in Manila a state-of-the-art institute for research and treatment.

The visitation at San Lazaro leprosarium was an experience I did not care to repeat. Leprosy is, if untreated, a very disfiguring disease. The facial tissues of the patients were in some cases so thickened that the features no longer appeared human. Many of them had lost fingers, toes, and other extremities, but the most horrible sight was the patient whose facial tissue became ulcerated to such an extent that the mid-portion of the face was entirely gone, so that the victim had neither a nose nor an upper lip. I diagnosed only two cases of leprosy while stationed at Sternberg. Both of these individuals were Philippine Scouts, and it was an unhappy chore to tell them the diagnosis. To these two men a diagnosis of leprosy was essentially a death sentence.

It is not reasonable to believe that the tropics and tropical assignments were to blame for everything which happened to members of the military in that setting. It is more reasonable to suppose that certain traits were present when one arrived, and that they were perhaps accentuated in the tropics. It has been proposed that some soldiers were shipped to the tropics to get them out of sight. One officer assigned to Sternberg, for reasons unknown to me, voluntarily spent at least eight years on the Philippine Islands. He was a well-trained specialist and very good at his job, but his behavior was, to say the least, bizarre. A bachelor who stayed pretty much to himself, he was never seen at the jai alai or in the Army-Navy Club. He loved flowers and spent a great deal of time working with the flowers on the hospital grounds. He waged a constant war against the insects and was occasionally seen talking to the flowers. Sometimes he was seen walking rapidly across the compound talking to himself. On one occasion as I was leaving the dependents' ward I saw the officer across the compound working with his flowers. Suddenly he ran a few steps and with a quick motion of his hand caught a large flying insect. The officer became very excited about the catch, and as I went by I heard him say, "Ah, ha! I got you that time," but he turned the bug loose and let it fly away.

I was excited and enthusiastic about my work at Sternberg. The officers with whom I worked were well trained, professional, and very pleasant. Except for our uniforms, we could have been working in a civilian hospital. This very happy atmosphere persisted until I had been at Sternberg for about eight weeks, and then an order came from somewhere that we uninitiated reserve officers must, since we had never had the advantage of being trained at Carlisle barracks, take the same courses in military medicine as the regular army officers had had at that place. Major William North, a regular army surgeon and a very fine officer (we secretly called him Uncle Willie), was handed the unpleasant task of administering these courses. Uncle Willie said, "I am very sorry, but the Army Medical Corps won't have it any other way." The course consisted almost entirely of homework. I had to take a bundle of sorry manuals home, study them, and fill out test papers. I do not believe these manuals had been revised since the Spanish-American War. We were supposed to learn the composition of two different kinds of army divisions, and further, we were supposed to learn about maps and the reading of war maps. Among other idiotic things, we were supposed to know the exact dimensions of and methods of digging an army privy. In spite of the "course" I enjoyed my work at Sternberg very much.

On the first of November 1941 the officers at Sternberg were assembled and told that henceforth they were not supposed to go home at noon and take a nap, or go out on the golf course, but were to stay in the hospital until 5:00 in the afternoon. It seemed that the War Department sensed a growing crisis and wished to prepare as much as possible. We continued this heightened schedule until December 7, 1941, the day of the attack on Pearl Harbor.

At Sternberg I came to know some unusual individuals whose reasons for being in the Philippine Islands were much more surprising than my own. I recall with great clarity one corpsman, James Marshall, who worked on one of my wards. James I found was a conscientious and professional worker. At times, however, he seemed far away, staring in my direction and not seeing me but looking past me at something too horrible to relate. At other times he would get a tormented look and behave like the Ancient Mariner, as if his burden were too heavy to carry alone. His story at times was clear, at other times rambling, disconnected, and rather wild. It was as if his thoughts were compelled to emerge through a small gate, and were in such current and counter current as to be almost totally unintelligible. I was able, after a few encounters, to piece together some of his story. In 1938, during the Spanish Civil War, he had become a member of the Lincoln Brigade, one of the Republican International Brigades which fought against General Franco's fascists. In the beginning he was such an idealist that he was easy to recruit. A victim of the great American Depression, he had led a nomadic existence until he found what he felt was the great cause – "fighting fascists."

At first he had believed that the cause of the Republican Army was just and that the heinous crimes committed were justified to accomplish the defeat of fascism. But when he witnessed, over many months, the senseless killing of thousands of innocents, his disillusionment came rapidly. He could not comprehend why people of the same race and same language could so ruthlessly murder each other. He saw mass executions committed by both sides. His own army burned churches, executing bishops and many hundreds of priests and religious leaders. Such horrors affected him so greatly that he deserted, left Spain by way of France, and returned to New York. Then, in 1940, for a lack of a job, he joined the army and soon found himself in the Philippines. At Sternberg, where he was working in a peaceful atmosphere, he became calmer and some of the haunted look went away.

From time to time I was given tasks in the hospital not related to my usual routine. On one occasion Major Gillespie called me into his office and asked me to go to the VIP suite on the Officers' Ward and do an electrocardiogram. Taking electrocardiograms was usually the job of Private McLean, and I had no idea why I should be called to do a private's work. Major Gillespie then told me that he wished me, after I had done the EKG, to do a history and physical. Usually the work on the Officers' Ward was done by a captain or major, but the officer on call for that ward was on sick leave. When I arrived at the Officers' Ward I saw a sign on the door which read "Do Not Disturb." Major Gillespie had not given me the name and rank of the patient before I left his office. When I entered the room, I saw a stocky man in pajamas lying on the bed staring at the ceiling. He had the appearance of someone who was totally exhausted and somewhat annoyed by the interruption, but he cooperated with me as I did his history and physical. This officer had been for many months assigned to Chungking, China, as a military observer. The city of Chungking was the object of repeated heavy bombing by the Japanese in 1938,

1939, 1940, and 1941. In 1941 the bombing had become almost incessant, and the officer had become so worn by the noise and destruction in Chungking that he could bear it no longer. He had no organic problem other than a moderately elevated blood pressure. Our objective at Sternberg was to help him rest and sleep for a few days until the first ship was available to transport him to the States. I escorted the general on board his ship for the voyage to San Francisco. He seemed much more serene and a lot less shaken than when he checked into Sternberg. The general had survived, but he was, as every other human, not built for such stress as he was subjected to in Chungking. I did not enter the diagnosis for the general's illness; this was done by the chief of the service at Sternberg. His condition was not unusual; thousands of men under such circumstances were diagnosed with combat fatigue.

We military who arrived in the Philippines were a varied lot. One individual I recall vividly; he was about 55 and looked much older. On account of his age and the fact that he had signed himself up as a urologist, he was given the rank of major. Apparently the army had not investigated the gentleman's credentials. The Philippine Department thought it was getting the services of a genitourinary surgeon. The truth was that the major had done some part-time work in a venereal disease clinic; among his colleagues at home he would be assigned the title of "Clap Doctor." The major was a very amiable, lovable sort of character, who had no family (his wife was dead) and who looked on this adventure in the exotic Philippines as the climax of his existence. Back home, according to his story, he was involved in many church and civic activities; even in the Philippines he linked up with the Manila Lions Club and became a regular church attender. His activities came prominently to the attention of the Philippine Department and the commanding officer at Sternberg, Colonel Cooper, when *The Manila Tribune* carried an article with star headlines which proclaimed that the major had given a talk at a civic club. The title of his speech was "The Prolongation of Longevity." His rank was much out of the range of his skills, and since the Philippine Department did not know how to use him, he was sent home. I am positive that this dear man would have accepted readily all of the hardships that were to come rather than to go home and miss his last chance at glory and acclaim, and I was sorry to see him go.

I am not sure whether Major Gillespie really liked my work at the

Pagsangan Falls, Luzon.

hospital or simply wanted to get me out of his sight, at least for a short while. He called me to his office one afternoon in August 1941 and told me that I was to go the next morning with a group of 20 convalescent soldiers on a recreational trip to Pagsangan Falls. Two of my charges were in casts and on crutches, and the remainder were recovering from malaria, dysentery, dengue, or some other tropical malaise. The trip was sponsored by the Philippine Red Cross and Mrs. Frances B. Sayres' Canteen Unit. Mrs. Sayres was the wife of the American High Commissioner in the Philippines. The bus for me and the soldiers was supplied by the Halili Transportation Company of Manila. The sponsoring women of Mrs. Sayres' Canteen Unit were responsible for the food, and that noon we were served food of such excellence that all of the convalescents ate an enormous amount. After the meal we military, but not the ladies, hiked to the falls. Pagsangan Falls, one of the main tourist attractions on Luzon, was a thrilling sight that lived up to its advance notices. On our way back from the falls we visited a Catholic church which seemed of almost cathedral proportions. As we came near we saw no one, and as we came nearer we saw that the massive doors were ajar. Around the entrance and piled against the door were leaves and other litter. We were startled as we entered the main sanctuary when a great number of bats flew out over our heads. The sanctuary in the dim light which entered through the stain glass windows was beautiful, but there was no one worshipping. The church was built in 1680 under Spanish rule, and one wondered just how many Filipinos working as slave labor and how many years it took to erect that magnificent structure, now apparently deserted.

When we got back to the lodge we were fed again. Those young men and I were given an outing which we could never forget. Unfortunately this was to be the last outing which 75 percent of my charges would ever have. I was proud of how well behaved and how courteous they were to our gracious hostesses.

At the late date of August 1941 there was, in general, no apparent feeling among the military of any proximate threat to our way of life in the Philippines. In spite of orders, most of the officers at Sternberg and elsewhere were working till noon and then taking off for the rest of the day for siesta, golf, the Army-Navy Club, or just relaxation. I recall brief comments about what was going on in China and in Europe, but the discussion never seemed to touch on any possible involvement of the U.S. forces in the Far East. *The Manila Tribune* was full of news about Douglas MacArthur's rebuilding of the Philippine Army, but this news was never linked to any sense of urgency.

While at Sternberg I continued to become acquainted more and more with some army personalities, all of whom contributed some different flavor to the peacetime army. One tall, skinny, sandy-haired young corporal with pale blue, shifty eyes was more obsequious than Uriah Heep. When I was officer of the day, "Uriah" could not grovel enough. Finally, privately, I asked the top sergeant what role the subservient corporal played in the scheme of things. The sergeant laughed and said that he thought everyone knew about the corporal. "He is a ten percenter," the sergeant answered. Just to prove my profound ignorance of things army, I asked, "What is a ten percenter?" And the sergeant explained that a ten percenter was one who lent money to his fellow soldiers until the next payday and for this short-term extension of credit received 10 percent interest. Since a large number of the enlisted men seemed to live as if there were no tomorrow, often spending the next fortnight's pay on the day that it was issued, there was nothing left to do, if one wanted a night on the town, but to seek out Uriah and obtain a loan. Uriah had his clients and was sure to get whatever was due him. I was indignant about this arrant usury. The next time that I was officer of the day I requested that the corporal be put on day duty (he did all of his banking at night, and had never been on day duty). He stayed on day duty for only two days; although I protested, the adjutant found my indignation very funny: "Lieutenant," he said, "don't you realize that the corporal and his ilk are very important to the army's scheme of things? He serves as a banker. They depend on it."

I recall one Saturday afternoon, soon after my arrival in the Philippines, when all officers and men were ordered to report to an auditorium on the 31st Infantry post within the walled city. There we were treated first to an ancient movie, then the entree for the evening. An officer with a pointer in his hand came on the stage and presented what I presumed was an army issue lecture on the prevention of VD (there was, and I suppose still is, an army manual for everything). The lecture, an unctuous exposition, was an insult to the intelligence of anyone. The lights were fortunately out, and it could not be determined who was giving our lecturer the raspberry. There were snorts, giggles, and outright guffaws. I do not know who was more relieved when that farce was over, the lecturer or me. This was a rite which had to be observed at intervals in order to fulfill army regulations.

At Sternberg, while the officers off duty could come and go as they pleased, the corpsmen were penned up in the hospital compound until they could get leave for a few hours. When those young men went out through the front gate at Sternberg, they were intent upon making the most of the opportunity. Many of them became so loaded with the product of the San Miguel Brewery that all of the ABCs of that lecture taken from the army manual were immediately forgotten and consequences meant nothing. They were 8,000 to 10,000 miles from home and in a strange land. Sternberg was a small enclave from which they escaped periodically to seek outlets for their pent-up energies.

Somehow on their return from leave these young men seemed much less buoyant than on their departure. Generally arriving en masse near midnight, all would report to the showers on Ward Six, where they would go through a routine called "prophylaxis." Most if not all of them had spent their evening at a house of doubtful repute, and all, whether a visitor to such a place or not, had to sign the book indicating that they had gone through the routine of prophylaxis. I suppose this practice was necessary since the incidence of venereal disease in the armed services in Manila was very high. One outfit stationed in Manila was unofficially reported to have an incidence of venereal disease of nearly 200 percent, meaning two fresh cases of VD per man per year. This figure seemed incredible to me, but the incidence by any method of reckoning was high. The army didn't seem to care what happened on leave, short of murder, arson, and rape, so long as one didn't run afoul of the law or return to the compound in such condition as to bring attention to oneself.

For a while as part of my training, I was required to sit for two to three hours in the enlisted men's barracks' office to observe how the medical corps operated when off duty. I was supposed to sit at the desk with the top sergeant and observe the everyday operations of the unit. On my second or third appearance, always on the weekend, I was so bored that I took a book along – one of the Hornblower trilogy by Forester. As I sat there immersed in my reading the following is presumed to have transpired: A sergeant came to the squad room with a first private in tow. The private was alleged to have been "skunk drunk" and very disorderly on his return from leave. The first sergeant was supposed to have written up the whole episode in my presence and under my keen observation. I did see the private come into the room, I did hear the buzz of conversation in the background, and I did see the sergeant depart with the young private. I heard nothing concerning the episode until about two weeks later, when I was advised that in two days I was to appear as a star witness in a court-martial case. I could not imagine why, and when I reported at the designated hour, I was no more informed than before. Having never attended a court-martial, I had a great deal of curiosity about such proceedings – especially about my role. There were a number of officers seated at a long table, and off at one side was a subdued, crestfallen young soldier, a private, who seemed vaguely familiar. Seated on his right was his counsel, and at another table was the prosecution. When the initial formalities were over, three to four corpsmen were called as witnesses, and I also vaguely remembered them in connection with some past event. I became very attentive when each of them began answering questions which related to the day and time when I had been an observer in the barracks' office. Each of them swore that the disconsolate young private had reported back to duty riotously inebriated and defiant of everything military, so much so that he had to be detained in the guardhouse.

I still wondered what all of this had to do with me. After the corpsmen had been questioned, it was my turn. I identified myself, and then I was asked whether on such and such a date I was present in the office of the corpsmen's barracks, and I replied in the affirmative. I was then asked if on such and such a date I had seen the private. My answer was yes, because I felt that he was one of several I saw on that date and in that place. The prosecutor then asked, "Was there anything unusual about his appearance and behavior?" I answered, most truthfully, "Not that I recall, sir." The entire panel of officers at the long table, the counsel, and the prosecutor, all gave me a shocked and incredulous look. The young man on trial, however, was absolutely agape. The prosecutor repeated the question in a more lengthy and detailed way as if to refresh my memory. Again my answer was "No, sir." There was again the dumbstruck response from all concerned, and I heard a few muffled snickers coming from behind me. There was a large turnout of off-duty officers and enlisted men at that trial. A court-martial was a rather rare event at Sternberg General

Hospital, and apparently those off duty were required to attend it as a training session. After my last answer the senior officer called the proceedings to order, and the case was dismissed for lack of evidence. As we left the room no one said a word to me, but there were many quizzical glances sent in my direction. I believe that C.S. Forester would have been delighted to know that young Horatio Hornblower could be so absorbing. Later, from curiosity, I made several inquiries about the dejected young private and finally had a chance to talk to him. He was from Texas where he had attended medical school for two years at Baylor. During his second year at Baylor he had had an unrequited love affair, and in his state of unhappiness he had left school and joined the army. The result was that the loss of his girl, leaving medical school, and finally being transported 10,000 miles from Texas had greatly compounded his misery. He was not really accustomed to any large alcoholic intake, and he had found that such overimbibing had made him become very belligerent. He intended to return home and go back to medical school when his stay in the army was over.

CHAPTER 6

Sternberg at War

December 7, 1941–January 7, 1942

On the morning of December 7, 1941, all was quiet in Manila. As usual we were sleeping late on Sunday morning, after partying the night before. I had looked forward to a quiet day in my quarters, but at about 8 A.M. (five and one-half hours after the beginning of the attack) I was awakened by a hand that shook me none too gently. I opened my eyes to see a stunned Lieutenant Ralph Hibbs. "John, wake up," he said. "The Japs have bombed Pearl Harbor." The expression on his face lent full credence to his words. As if I were sleepwalking, I got out of bed, dressed, and ate breakfast. Dominidor served us in complete silence. Our prolonged, pleasant stay in a tropical paradise had just ended.

After breakfast I walked down beautiful, flame tree–lined Gral

Luna Boulevard to Sternberg Hospital. Everyone I saw that morning, both on and off the wards, was visibly shaken by the news, and my own state of shock was not improved when I recalled that it was a year to the day since I had been called on active duty. I had been promised that I should be released from the armed forces in time to arrive home on December 7, 1941. I should have been eating Sunday morning breakfast with my parents in North Carolina.

The news of the bombing, however, was just a faint indication of what was to come. In a very few hours we learned that Clark Field had been bombed heavily (about noon) and that we would soon be getting casualties – severe ones, and in a much greater number than we were prepared to handle. Following Clark Field, Cavite Navy Yard, Fort McKinley, and Corregidor had all come under heavy bombardment. Many of the injured had wounds which the hospital was totally unprepared to receive and treat. There were severe head and chest wounds presented at our door for which there were neither specialists nor equipment to treat. We had neither a neurosurgeon nor a chest surgeon on our roster at Sternberg.

Soon after Cavite Navy Yard was bombed, a young lieutenant commander was brought in on a stretcher with a gasping, sucking wound of his right chest. We were no more prepared to care for him than we were to orbit the moon. Without even a bed to put him in, we placed him on the floor in a hallway and gave him an injection of morphine. I passed the young man several times in the next hour or two. He did not groan, complain, or call out. Though I saw many who were equally distressed, this young naval officer was fixed in my memory forever – such courage I had never seen. I stopped two or three times, knowing I could do nothing but ask if I could help in any way. He was gasping for breath and in great pain, but each time he smiled, "There's nothing you can do." As I came back by him sometime later, he was gone, his eyes open wide, looking at something 10,000 miles away: home.

Incredibly, Sternberg, the only military general hospital in the Philippines, had no emergency room. The single room in the front part of the hospital inappropriately called an emergency room was fitted for sick call only. As the glut of injured patients came to us, we had only floors and hallways on which to place them. Our surgeons quietly, capably, and efficiently took care of what we would ordinarily call general surgery, but brain and thoracic surgery were beyond their ken. Most of the equipment of the hospital was unbelievably outdated. There was one ice-cooled oxygen tent, but there were no oxygen outlets on the walls of the hospital rooms. Though more such equipment may have been stored in warehouses, it was not set up in the hospital when needed. December 7 was the beginning of a long nightmare.

At the end of the first day, I went back to my quarters, filled one musette bag with what I considered essential, and reported back to the hospital. After that I ate when I could and slept where I could find a spot to lie down.

On the morning of the second day after Pearl Harbor we were faced with another horrible scene. The docks on the waterfront had become secondary targets; one of the worst hit was the quartermaster laundry, which was almost completely staffed with Chinese workers. Soon after the laundry was hit and its scalding steam released from fragmented pipes, we received a great influx of the afflicted workers with ghastly burns. There were no beds for them, so those poor souls were laid out on the grass and concrete in front of the surgical building. In spite of extensive third degree burns, those Chinese, except for an occasional muted moan, were impassive and uncomplaining. We cared for them where they lay, on the ground or on the concrete. First, we gave each an injection of morphine. To expose the burned areas we had to remove their shirts, pants, and underclothes with scissors. On many of the victims, extensive fluid-filled blebs adhered so strongly to their clothes that in the process of cutting away and removing their clothes we pulled away large blebs of skin filled with fluid. With burns covering 60 to 70 percent of their bodies, several looked like large weeping sores. All the while they wore the stolid, stoical expression of those who accept what comes as fated. Compared to the treatment modes of the present, our handling of those cases was primitive. We had fluids, glucose and saline, and there was sulfanilamide for infection. We also used tannic acid and gentian violet, applied as a coating to the denuded areas. In spite of all our efforts, several died of shock, toxemia due to extensive tissue injury, and infection. At that time I recalled from my several months of experience in a children's hospital that we nursed burnt patients, debrided their burned areas, fought infections, and spent seemingly endless hours taking little divots of skin from an unburned area and applying it to the burned one – all this for weeks and months under the best conditions.

The flood of patients was greatest in the first three to four days. Thereafter the steady flow of the sick and wounded kept us very busy.

I had just about forgotten James Marshall, but a few days after the war began I saw him again on ward six where he performed his duties in an exceptional manner, although his haunted far-off look had returned. I wondered at that time if he would be able to survive mentally under wartime conditions. At least he was now helping people instead of being part of the group engaged in random slaughter. I tried very hard to reassure him but did not feel that my words were of any help.

On about the third day after the onset of hostilities we engaged, by executive order, in a futile exercise. From day one the hospital had been clearly marked so that there could be no mistaking its identity. However, the administration did not trust the Japanese. Reports from China indicated that the Japanese were bombing hospitals, with no regard for the Geneva Convention. Corpsmen were ordered to dig trenches, and in short order a gaping wound criss-crossed the beautiful hospital quadrangle. Much of the exotic shrubbery and many trees were destroyed, but such is war. The Japanese planes flew singly and in formation at any level they chose, facing no opposition whatever. The Japanese knew the entire island from the years of unhindered spying, but there were a score or more targets on the islands of Luzon and Corregidor which were much more profitable for them to strike. No bombs came nearer to Sternberg than the Pasig River, at least while we remained at the hospital, but every time the bombers came over, sirens went off and everyone not involved in an emergency was supposed to dive into a foxhole or trench. In the beginning, most of us followed orders, but after the first two days sirens were going off so often that all but a faithful few became bored with that routine.

There were, however, those who continued to observe reflexively the practice of diving into a trench on signal. In the very early days of the air raids I was standing just in front of the surgery when an alarm went off. I observed a young army nurse dive into a trench, and then just after she had disappeared from view a young corpsman came rushing across the compound and dived into the trench squarely on top of her. Instantly, there was an eruption from that trench – he as if propelled, she immediately following like wasps when their nest is struck with a rock. The young nurse had worked on my wards for months, and I had thought of her as very quiet, pleasant, demure, and extremely efficient; but on this occasion she was none of the above. What issued from that usually sedate, controlled young lady was pure Billingsgate. The young corpsman beat a hasty retreat, and when the young nurse looked around and saw that there was an audience, she too disappeared in short order. I saw this young lady several times afterwards, both at Sternberg General Hospital and on Bataan, but never so flustered!

After a few days none of us hit the trenches, no matter how many planes nor how low they flew. We were observing blackouts and the trenches became a menace; several people stumbled into the trenches in the dark. Fortunately no one was badly injured.

On the third or fourth day something happened which was entirely unfitted to our role as medical personnel; the executive officer issued to every medical officer a shiny new .45 automatic pistol, army issue. I had never seen one before, and I had no idea how to load or fire it. I accepted it very gingerly, and when the exec had gone I put that toy in my desk drawer, reflecting that in the long list of items we desperately needed to run a hospital in wartime, an automatic pistol was not high on the list. We kept the pistols for two days until a major in the Medical Corps, Reserve, began firing at a formation of Japanese bombers 15,000 feet overhead. After that episode the executive recovered the sidearms much faster than he had issued them, muttering all the while that those guns were much more of a menace to us than they were to the enemy.

On the fifth or sixth day, Colonel Gillespie ordered me to go with an ambulance and driver to a Filipino hospital about 80 miles north of Manila. I was to pick up Colonel Charles L. Steele, commander of the 31st Infantry. He had developed severe pneumonia while in the field with his regiment. No transportation was available to take him to Manila, so he was placed temporarily in a Philippine civilian hospital. My driver, a private in the Philippine Scouts, knew the countryside well, having been on maneuvers over most of Luzon before the war. The Japanese Air Force, after the first few hours of the war, were practically unopposed, and their fighter planes were flying low and leisurely over the countryside looking for prey.

Over this main north-south highway the planes were inquisitive about anything that moved. Even though our ambulance had a red cross on top of it, we really did not trust the Japanese. As we went along the highway, two or three planes approached. Each time they came near and flew low, we would duck off the road into a clump of trees. It took us hours to get to the civilian hospital. On the way back, the colonel, the private, and I decided that the trees were no protection and that we should just high-tail it back to Manila. We were all relieved to reach Sternberg.

As the days passed we continued to get casualties. Some of the sick and wounded could be returned to duty, but we were receiving more each day than we were discharging. Some large warehouse-like buildings near the Pasig River were filled with beds and used for the convalescent. There were rumors from the incoming casualties that the Japanese were advancing in northern Luzon and that all armed forces would be retreating into Bataan where we were to make a stand. There was also a rumor that a hospital ship under some sort of truce would be allowed to sail from Manila to Australia with all of the patients who had no possibility of returning to duty. In time of war the rumor mill grinds incessantly, and those revelations could not be sorted out until proven by the event.

Until December 23 I had not been back to my own quarters. When I returned on that date I found that my suitemates, lieutenants Hibbs, Saldivar, and Kaufmann, had left several days before. Dominidor was still there guarding against possible looting by his own people. I had few possessions except for some winter uniforms, several books, some pictures, and an ancient, beat-up Corona typewriter. I had a difficult time making decisions, but I could take only what I could put into a duffel bag and leave the rest behind. I chose, fortunately, socks, underwear, and a couple of tropical uniforms. Dominidor stood glumly by, voicing his deep concern about what would happen to his family after the Americans left Manila. I had no way of reassuring him. He had heard about the Japanese atrocities against the civilians in Nanking and elsewhere in China. I told Dominidor that he was welcome to everything which I was leaving behind, then bade him goodbye and returned to Sternberg.

The Japanese ground assault on Luzon began on December 10 and had moved swiftly and inexorably toward Manila. On December 24 General MacArthur ordered the implementation of War Plan Orange, the strategic retreat to the 30-mile by 15-mile peninsula of Bataan. Having overestimated the capabilities of his forces, however, MacArthur waited almost too long to give the order so that the retreat took place under the worst possible conditions. Some 80,000 American and Philippine forces hurriedly withdrew to Bataan in the face of a two-front attack, struggling to gather scattered food, ammunition, and medical supplies as they went. Declaring Manila an open city (although the Japanese bombed and shelled it anyway), MacArthur withdrew his staff and family to the fortress island of Corregidor off the tip of the peninsula of Bataan.

On the night before the Sternberg staff withdrew, I was officer of the day. One of the duties of the officer of the day was to play obstetrician to the wives of the Philippine Scouts and enlisted men. At about 11 P.M. of December 24, I was called to the delivery room where a young Filipino woman seemed about to deliver. I had not delivered a baby since my senior year in medical school. My last call on outside obstetrics at the Medical College of Virginia had been in Shocko Valley, where I was called on, along with Irene Levy, another senior medical student, to attend a female who made her distress call much too early. We waited and waited in that filthy hovel, and that baby showed no signs of arriving. We called the obstetrical resident and told him what the situation was. "Come on in, you dopes," he said. "You should have left there five hours ago." This incident illustrates my lack of obstetrical expertise.

When I arrived in the delivery room at Sternberg, a captain in the Army Nursing Corps, an old hand at the game, cheered me on. She could have done the job much better than I. Her witticisms as I continued my clumsy efforts were not at all reassuring. I was comforted to know that there was a proper head down position of the fetus. That baby took about three hours to arrive, and all the while my coach, the nurse, was saying, "Hold it back, don't let it come too fast." I was tempted to ask her to come to the action end of that table and take my place. When the baby finally emerged, its cranium had molded so much that its head was about twice normal length. I have thought many times since about that child and hope that he survived the terrible ordeal of the war. I have also wondered how much my ineptitude as an obstetrician may have affected his IQ. I tried, since I felt sure that he might be my last delivery, to pressure his mother into letting me name the baby; but she, who seemed to be happy having a baby even in such perilous times, insisted that he be named José Ramirez.

After delivering José, I was able to lie down and rest intermittently, although I could hear clearly the rumble of tanks and heavy guns withdrawing from the city. The next morning we were told that in the evening the staff of Sternberg would meet in front of the headquarters building to prepare for departure for Bataan, where we were to set up a field hospital. Sternberg had been left in charge of Colonel Percy J. Carroll, Lieutenant Florence McDonald, eight Filipino civilian doctors, and eight Filipino civilian nurses. Manila Bay had been bombed so heavily that by the end of December only one ship was still afloat, the inter-island ship *Macatan*, which was being converted into a hospital ship for the evacuation of the Sternberg patients. The *Macatan* was to take them to Australia.

The chief medical officer had requested permission, through channels, for the Japanese to permit safe passage, but had received no reply. From my knowledge of the patients' conditions, I judged that many would have little chance for survival under the best of circumstances and that staying in Manila would mean certain death for many of them. Thus 224 sick and wounded Americans and Filipinos were placed on board the *Macatan*. After the war we learned that the ship, after great trials but with no loss of life, had reached Sydney, where the patients were then hospitalized.

We gathered after dark, as scheduled, in front of the hospital headquarters. From our commanding officer Lieutenant Colonel William "Rhiney" Craig down to the lowest rank, we were a dejected outfit; we were, in a sense, retreating. As we sat or stood there we heard the flapping of wings. A very large bird lit just above the cornice at the edge of the roof of the headquarters. Some said it was an eagle, but the only thing I could be sure of was that even the bird seemed dispirited. We did not speak of its being a possible evil omen. When any one of us would try to scare the bird away, we heard only a languid, slow flapping of its wings. Probably sick or injured, the bird did nothing to elevate our mood. Finally our transportation came, and we began to wind our way through the dark deserted streets of Manila to the docks. Only the moon, in the presence of a blackout, lit our going.

When we arrived at the docks, we were told that we would cross Manila Bay in a small freighter, which was still being loaded when we arrived at the dock. Lieutenant Colonel Craig was in charge. Soon the loading of cargo was finished; and we medical officers, nurses, and corpsmen boarded with only the moonlight to aid us. We soon learned that there were no staterooms; we had to lie, sit, or stand on deck. In the darkness there was much stumbling around and a bit of swearing as we bruised our shins. By the time we had staked out a claim for space on the deck, each person had a spot just large enough to lie down in but not to turn over. There was no sorting out in regard to rank or sex. The Executive Officer announced that there was a communal toilet below deck and that ladies would go first. This announcement caused further scrambling and confusion; everyone wanted to go at once. After quite a while the male contingent was able to go below; that night I understood the rationale for having a two-to-one ratio of women's toilet facilities to men's at a football stadium. I was very grateful for having a society bladder.

The boat finally got under way, moving slowly and quietly in the darkness amid the bombed-out boats in the dock. We had to wind our way through what seemed to be a ghost fleet. After we had cleared the immediate harbor and its fleet of sunken hulls, someone began in a low voice to sing, and slowly more voices were added until all were singing or humming. None of the provinces on the east, Manila side of the bay nor Bataan on the west side had yet fallen into the hands of the Japanese, so our music was heard by friendly ears. We proceeded almost directly due west. Part of the time we heard the muted sound of the engine, and at other times the boat seemed to be drifting with only the sound of water slapping against the hull. We proceeded so slowly that we did not dock at Limay, a small shallow port on the east side of Bataan, until just after daybreak. As we started to go ashore, Colonel Craig made it known that the boat had to be unloaded. We had not known it, but when we left Manila we were carrying some of the supplies needed to set up General Hospital #2. Since there were obviously no stevedores around, it was quite clear who would unload the boat.

The nurses were sent on their way by bus either to General Hospital #1 or to General Hospital #2, both of which were being set up. Soon after we had docked, three Japanese bombers began a lazy, low circling of the area. The ship was clearly marked as medical, but that did not relieve our feeling of unease. Then the planes began to make bomb runs directly at us. No bomb came within 400 yards of the boat, and we never knew whether they meant business or were just toying with us, but it was difficult to unload a boat and keep one eye on the heavens at the same time. Colonel Craig set a great example; he stood in the middle of the deck giving orders and never once paid the least attention to the bombers above. I both envied and admired his cool aplomb, but I was inherently unsuited for such a role. Finally we were able to complete the unloading.

Other than the nurses, the officers and men were taken to a hillside above Limay, where we were to spend the night sleeping on the ground with nothing between us and the grass but a blanket. Before I went to sleep, a Philippine Scout, Sergeant Morales, came by. He recognized me because I had taken care of his little daughter at Sternberg General Hospital, where she had been treated for a kidney disorder (glomerulonephritis). She had improved, and both the sergeant and his wife had seemed very grateful for what they supposed I had done. When he recognized me on that hillside, he was very solicitous of my well-being and wanted me to take part of his bedding roll to make a pillow for myself. Of course, I could not permit such sacrifice on his part.

The sergeant was representative of the demeanor of all the Philippine Scouts whom I encountered. They were polite, pleasant, and always soldierly. The Scouts, of which there were two regiments, were never allowed to rise above the rank of an NCO; they were paid one-half the stipend given an American soldier of equivalent rank. These men were real professionals, but they were treated like second class citizens in their own country. I never saw the sergeant again, and I have often wondered what happened to him and his little daughter.

At about sunup on the morning of December 24, Captain Jack Comstock, Captain Harold Bertram, and I were asked to go to General Hospital #1, located just on the bay near Limay. The hospital was set up in some old barracks buildings which were just shells with rough splintered floors and sawali roofs. The operating room, in a 14 by 20 foot frame building, was said to have been a barroom prior to the war. Equally dilapidated buildings had been converted into a kitchen, a headquarters building, and a laboratory. My ward, 20 by 60 feet, held 15 single cots on either side of a narrow aisle; the nurses' station was in the rear. In front and on the right as one entered the building was a single room about 8 by 10 feet which had been used as an office or quarters of a platoon sergeant. To my amazement, as I opened the door, I found the room full of Seth Thomas clocks. I wondered later why with such a great lack of everything else we were blessed with such an excess of clocks. Perhaps this was a reflection of USAFFE (United States Armed Forces in the Far East) war plans. After the war started, for example, a medical supply depot containing a large supply of fine binocular microscopes was discovered, whereas the lab at Sternberg General Hospital had had only some old beat-up monocular scopes.

My patients on that ward at General Hospital #1 were not war casualties from Bataan but patients evacuated from Manila by the overland route. They were, in general, men who were presumed to be able later to return to duty. My ward, purely non-surgical, was filled largely with soldiers suffering from malaria and dysentery. Combat troops had not yet retreated to Bataan, so there were as yet few wounded being admitted.

Christmas Day at General Hospital #1 was relatively quiet, at least quiet enough for us to enjoy our holiday meal. At noon that day, December 25, 1941, we were to enjoy our last bountiful meal for years. We ate turkey and ham with all the trimmings. Colonel Duckworth, the commandant of the hospital, presided at the main table; he hinted that from now on we were not to expect to be fed in this manner. He was right: almost within a day we were told we were being cut to two meals a day and put on half rations.

Colonel James W. Duckworth was a no-nonsense officer who was ideally suited by training, experience, and dominating physical presence to command a hospital in the field. He would brook no difference in opinion, especially if that opinion was counter to his own. Some of my colleagues had warned me about the colonel's ungiving nature, so I was careful that none of my words or actions ran contrary to his.

For lack of other means of transportation, some of the supplies and vehicles were brought overland. A few of the corpsmen had volunteered to drive some much-needed ambulances on the main highway north from Manila to San Fernando, and then westward to the main highway which led down the east coast to Bataan. On New Year's Day, when those ambulances arrived at San Fernando, the city was burning, under bombardment, and Japanese troops were on the outskirts of the city. Some of the vehicles had been driven through such intense heat that their paint was peeling. When the ambulances arrived at General Hospital #1, the drivers were acclaimed for their exploits. One driver, Private Bonk, a brash red-headed lad from Brooklyn, was not in the least shaken by his adventure. When I asked him if he had not been afraid on his mad adventure, he replied, "Nah, I wasn't afraid; I had me gat" (gun). Being a noncombatant, he was soon relieved of his "gat."

General Hospital #1 in the very early days did not receive a great number of front-line casualties, but after New Year's there was a rapid increase in the influx of sick and wounded. Although I was not a surgeon, I was called to the operating room to assist in whatever way I could. I felt inadequate in a surgical setting. The seven or eight operating tables crowded the poorly equipped, 14 by 40 foot operating room. Pressure cookers were used for sterilizers. The windows were wide open and winged insects flew in and around the lights over the operating table. Dust drifted into the operating room each time an ambulance or truck passed by on the dirt road outside. The tables were always occupied with patients, some of whom were horribly wounded in the head, chest, and abdomen. I was surprised at the number of eye injuries. I stood at one table where enucleations (removal of the eyeball) were performed on one patient after another. There seemed to be no eye injury so slight that the eye could be saved.

At that time General Hospital #1 had no neurosurgeon and no thoracic surgeon. The operating surgeons, save one eye surgeon, were general surgeons who worked very hard to save lives. The surgeons, as I recall, were Captain Alfred Weinstein, Colonel Frank Adamo, and Colonel John L. Schlock. Captain Weinstein, the most flamboyant of the surgeons, had a flair and passion in his work, operating like one possessed. Such skill and speed were necessary, since as soon as one casualty left the table, another took his place. In the neverending procession of wounded, there was no time for the real niceties of surgery. The objective of all concerned was to save lives. Many limbs were lost because of an immediate need to amputate. Time and a good vascular surgeon could have saved many extremities, but of course we did not have a vascular surgeon.

Amid such a torrent of the badly wounded, the demand for blood increased. In our beleaguered situation, there was no outside source of blood. The only blood available was that which flowed in the circulation of the staff of General Hospital #1. The officers and enlisted men were constantly being canvassed to find more donors, and some of the staff gave two to three units in a relatively short period of time. Giving so much blood in a short period of time when on half rations was a sacrifice, but the need was so great that I knew of no one who refused. Considerable plasma had been brought into Bataan and issued to the hospital; when there was no blood available, plasma was used in the operating room and on the surgical wards. We did not realize until much later that some of that plasma was infected, and a considerable number of patients became ill with hepatitis.

Although General Hospital #1 was clearly marked as a hospital, we did not trust the Japanese, and we proceeded to dig slit trenches. The Japanese planes did come over, and they did bomb and strafe, but it was always outside the compound, usually targeting some quartermaster buildings nearby. When the siren went off somewhere in the neighborhood, the doctors, nurses, and corpsmen in the operating room could not leave and jump into a trench and neither could many of the very ill or those in traction. Finally almost everyone came to ignore the siren. I gave orders on my ward that everyone should stay in bed or on the ward when the alarm went off, but I had one patient on my ward, a young private from the 31st Infantry, who in spite of all orders would dive out of the ward and into a trench when the alarm went off. I remonstrated with him repeatedly but to no avail. Finally he said, "Captain, I hear you, I understand you, and I try to obey you, but when I hear those planes and that siren my legs just won't obey me."

There were not a great many Japanese prisoners taken in Bataan. It was the code of the Japanese that one was disgraced by being taken prisoner and that it was more honorable to fight to the death. I saw only one Japanese prisoner while in Bataan, a young enlisted man who was picked up badly wounded during a skirmish at the front and brought in by ambulance. After his arrival, he was treated by the surgeons and placed in a small room under guard. I was asked by the adjutant to accompany him on a visit to our captive and try to determine what the prisoner's needs were. In response to our inquiries, made with signs and gestures, he gave no evidence that he understood any of our efforts at communication. He just lay there and viewed us with unblinking malevolence. He had been taught that if one were captured he could not return, except in disgrace. I believe he would have preferred dying at the front rather than being in our care. In our presence he never took a sip of any liquid or a single bite of food, although on our next visit his food would be gone. Perhaps he felt that if he did not eat in our presence it was the same as if he had not eaten at all. After his wounds healed, this particular prisoner was taken elsewhere to a stockade and kept till the fall of Bataan.

The number of patients coming into General Hospital #1 at the beginning depended on the intensity of the fighting at the front. Throughout the two weeks that I was at General Hospital #1, there was a steady flow of the sick and wounded into our ward.

CHAPTER 7

General Hospital #2, Bataan

January 7, 1942–April 9, 1942

Around January 7, 1942, several nurses and doctors, mostly those who had been at Sternberg General Hospital, were ordered to go to General Hospital #2, set up in the jungle about two miles south and east of Cabcaben, three miles east of the bay, and about eight miles southeast of Limay. We were transported there in some commandeered Batangas buses. As I left my ward, I picked up one of those Seth Thomas clocks I had discovered. It was government property, and I should have filled out a requisition, but in that setting a lot of government red tape was forgotten.

The eight miles or so from General Hospital #1 at Limay to General Hospital #2 seemed much longer over a rutty, bumpy road, but our spirits were high. We were happy to leave the chaotic situation at Hospital #1, even for the totally unknown. General Hospital #2 was situated just south of, and on the slopes of, Mt. Bataan. The hospital setting was in the jungle astride the Real River and on the lower slopes of the mountain. The Real River hardly qualified as a river, since it was only about 12 to 15 feet wide and very shallow, but it was a very important stream as far as the hospital was concerned. It was the source of every drop of our drinking, bathing, and cooking water. After being chlorinated and filtered, the water was stored in a 3,000 gallon tank.

Arriving at General Hospital #2, I found that its headquarters was at the base of a huge banyan tree whose large flat roots projected about 18 to 24 inches above the ground. Colonel James O. Gillespie, commanding officer of the hospital, and Lieutenant Colonel Craig had their sleeping quarters between the roots of this tree. When I reported, I presented the Seth Thomas clock to Colonel Gillespie. He never asked me where I got it; he did nail it on the tree, and it was thereafter the official timepiece of General Hospital #2. Captain Jack Comstock and I put our blankets, mosquito nets, and other supplies on a flat area just a few feet from the Real River. On Bataan we had no worries about poisonous snakes or spiders. The real enemy was the mosquito, and Bataan was a veritable hotbed of malaria.

The hospital was spread out for a couple of kilometers along the Real. The headquarters was almost in the center of the compound. The nurses' quarters, just across the river, were a large roofless area, enclosed with a wall of burlap to provide some privacy. (They had raided a nearby quartermasters building for a large hamper of burlap bags and had sewn them together to make a wall.) In addition, some large abandoned buses had been renovated as sleeping quarters for the nurses.

Fortunately, about 400 yards east of headquarters and flowing down from the slopes of Mt. Bataan over a rock cliff into the Real were some cool and brisk waterfalls. The nurses had their designated times to use the falls and the river for bathing and washing their clothes. It is not recorded that anyone of the male gender ever intruded on the nurses' private hours at the falls.

The main north-south highway ran just east and south of the hospital, and many weary, tired, dusty, dirty military men drifted into the hospital for a bath at the falls. A great number of those officers were, for a short period of time, able to stop off to rid themselves of the dust and grime. The north-south road was dirt, and it was the dry season. Each vehicle passing on that trail raised a billowing cloud of suffocating dust. I recall vividly one visitor to the falls, Major Joseph McCloskey of the Medical Corps, who dropped in to visit and take a shower under the falls. It was late evening, and I had a little earlier left my ward to take a shower and eat in the officers' mess. Just after I disrobed and got under that falls, the major, a perfect stranger, came in to start his bath. He was a handsome, well-built young man of 35 to 38, who seemed to have something very serious on his mind. We exchanged only a few words, but he did introduce himself as Major Joseph McCloskey. Later that evening as we gathered under the clock at the big tree, someone mentioned a tragedy. On his way back to his outfit, Major McCloskey had been killed by a Japanese bomber. I learned later that he was the first American medical officer killed in the Philippine Islands. After his death an army general hospital was named after him.

I was assigned to Ward #2, just south and west of the receiving ward. My good friends Captain Jack Comstock and Colonel William "Uncle Willie" North worked there. My ward, a medical ward, was in a clearing surrounded by a thicket of shrubs, underbrush, and bamboo. In the beginning the ward held only 100 patients, mostly victims of malaria and dysentery. Each patient had a cot, a mattress, and two blankets. In the perimeter of the ward were pit toilets and a lister bag of chlorinated water. The toilets were slit trenches dug precisely to Army Medical Corps specifications, each having a superstructure of a pole to roost on while one performed that needed function.

The nurses' station, run by Lieutenant Mary Jo Oberst, was in a small tent which held the charts and a meager supply of medication. In the first three or four weeks my patient population continued with the same problems that had been prevalent at General Hospital #1: malaria and dysentery. When those young soldiers first arrived in Bataan, they were healthy and well nourished. After three to four weeks of heavy fighting, though, the diet, inadequate both in quantity and quality, began to have an effect. Their rations during combat could not be relied on to arrive on time, if at all. Their sources of drinking water were frequently contaminated. At times when thirsty, the soldiers—especially those from the Philippine army—would drink from a stream or pond—never inquiring what was upstream. Additionally, there were days when they were under attack and could not get any rest. So after February 1 we began to get steadily increasing numbers of patients who, in addition to the malaria and dysentery, had also developed signs of malnutrition, were much sicker than before, and were much more difficult to return to duty.

One incident, I believe in mid–February 1942, is stuck indelibly in my memory. My ward was only 200 to 300 yards from the receiving ward where Lieutenant Colonel William North and Captain Jack Comstock were in charge, and I frequently had a need to consult with Jack about a patient he had sent to my ward. On one occasion as I approached his station, I saw Jack talking to a soldier who was almost hysterical. As I came nearer I saw that he was not an American, and neither did he have the fine, more chiseled features of a Filipino. He looked Japanese. He was explaining to Captain Comstock in poor English that he had just recently joined a Philippine army unit where he was a stranger and where his comrades in arms had threatened to kill him because they thought him to be Japanese and a spy. The Filipino soldiers were hearing terrible stories about what was happening to their families on Luzon and in Manila, and they hated anything that resembled a Japanese. The young soldier was pleading with Jack to admit him to give him sanctuary. Captain Comstock tried as well as he could to explain to the young soldier that the rules did not permit him to admit anyone for such a purpose, and the young soldier was compelled to return to his unit. Later that day when I left my ward to go to the mess for the evening meal, I passed the receiving ward, and as I came near the station I saw a very still figure lying on a stretcher. As I approached, the face and figure became much more familiar. I saw with shock that it was the young Filipino soldier who was unfortunate enough to resemble a Japanese. He had been shot by someone in his own unit and had died on the way to the hospital.

The surgical cases after January 10 arrived in steadily increasing numbers, but in early February there was, for many reasons, a steady and ever increasing stream of medical cases. Packed on the peninsula were some 80,000 troops and 26,000 civilians who were carrying, because of the hasty retreat, less than a month's supply of food. Malnutrition was making its appearance.

The siege began with General MacArthur ordering everyone on half rations, fewer than 2,000 calories per day – a starvation diet under the circumstances. After February 15 came a slow but steady decrease in the calorie count of the food. Under front line conditions the food was even worse than that in the hospital, which itself was exceedingly bad. The bulk of our food at the hospital was milled rice, lacking in all vitamin content. During late January and the first two weeks of February we were given some occasional servings of carabao meat, which had to be slaughtered, cooked, and served all on the same day since there was no refrigeration. We got an occasional serving of salmon but never any fresh fruit or vegetables. By March 12, when General MacArthur reluctantly left Corregidor for Australia, the garrison was on one-third rations; by April 3, when the Japanese began their final push, the garrison was on one-fourth rations.

From the very beginning, medical supplies were short as well. There was not enough quinine for both prophylaxis and treatment. Because of this shortage, even when it was used for acute malaria, quinine was given in inadequate doses. The need for quinine steadily increased. By late February some units in the combat area had a 70 to 80 percent incidence of malarial infections. One of the reasons so many soldiers, especially of the Philippine army, developed malaria was that they had either abandoned or lost their mosquito nets. This usually happened during retreat, when they abandoned their supplies. By the end of February we were getting hundreds of cases per day of malaria and dysentery. The cases of malaria were frequently very severe. Although our laboratory was headed by an excellent pathologist, Captain Harold Keschner, he and his assistants could not possibly run malaria smears on all patients. On request they checked the worst cases. A surprising number of soldiers had two to three different types of malaria parasites floating in their bloodstream. During the campaign malaria and other tropical diseases were to take more casualties than the Japanese.

In spite of using a mosquito net and taking one tablet a day of quinine as prophylaxis, I wound up with a clinical, almost incapacitating, malaria. The pathologists found both tertian and quartan malaria in my bloodstream. My chills, my aches, and my febrile episodes were totally unpredictable, but compared to many of the rest, my own case of malaria was relatively mild.

Numerous and persistent, the big blue flies undoubtedly were the chief carriers of the enteric diseases. A general lack of sanitation and open pit toilets formed a fertile breeding ground for them. We had to eat when the air was thick with flies, usually waving with one hand while eating with the other.

There were several cases of cerebral malaria, generally caused by the most virulent type of parasite, plasmodium falciparium. Infection by this parasite carries a high mortality. I saw at least two manifestations of this more lethal strain of the disease. These cases generally arrived in the hospital after several days of no, or inadequate, treatment. The patient was generally in a comatose or semi-comatose state, with a high fever and chills. In the early phase, before the onset of coma, patients complained of terrible headaches. In the more severe and often fatal cases, paralysis occurred. There was also a manifestation called oculogyrics which we see rarely in the United States, a rapid, irregular movement of the eyes which seems to have no particular pattern. In spite of our best efforts, I had to watch a sergeant who had served with me at Sternberg die from cerebral malaria. Not as dramatic but equally deadly was the form of pernicious malaria called black water fever. This form of malaria was also caused by the falciparium parasite. In black water fever the clinical manifestations were jaundice, dark urine, and collapse. The chills and fever were totally unpredictable in their timing. Fortunately the incidence of these two complications was not high, but when black water fever occurred it was very often fatal.

For cerebral malaria and black water fever we did have some intravenous quinine. The malaria itself was made much more deadly by the presence of dysentery and malnutrition. At least 80 percent of the patients admitted to my ward had malaria, and of these more than 50 percent had chronic or acute diarrhea. We never had enough personnel in the lab to test stools on everyone, so one could not be sure whether we were dealing with bacteria or amoebae as the infective agents. In the front lines were soldiers, especially of the Philippine army, who unfortunately would eat anything, good or bad, when they were hungry. The Philippine army was made up largely of raw recruits who had had but a few weeks training and had not been taught the elements of self-preservation in the jungle. They had also a very high incidence of intestinal parasites including hookworm and roundworm. I had known from my experience at Sternberg General Hospital that a high percentage of the Philippine Scouts and their dependents had intestinal parasites, at times two to three varieties. This added factor no doubt contributed to the diarrhea problem. By late January many were being admitted to the ward with diarrhea, acute and chronic, with the added problem of malnutrition and malaria.

Overt signs of vitamin deficiency in General Hospital #2 began to appear several weeks after the beginning of the starvation diet. Some were able to delay the deficiency with occasional small feedings of native peas, salmon, and carabao meat. On the other hand, malnutrition was hastened by the fact that the diet was largely carbohydrates, specifically milled rice. The pericarp of cereal grains contains nearly all of the B-complex vitamins, and when this layer is removed by milling there is little left but carbohydrate.

In my experience, there was no deficiency which presented itself as a pure entity. Generally there were manifestations of several B-complex deficiencies, appearing in phases. Any individual afflicted with a deficiency of any part of the B complex of vitamins was absolutely sure to have at least some evidence, in a varying degree, of deficiency in other moieties of the B array. The diet at all times was woefully deficient, and all the evidences of this problem in late January 1942 were only a prelude to what was to come in February, March, and early April when General Hospital #2 was overwhelmed by a crushing number of very ill men coming in from the front lines. Not only did they come in increasing numbers, but they were progressively more starved, more emaciated, and more infected with malaria. Some of these troops had been, without relief for weeks on end, before they arrived at the hospital. There was in fact no relief available, either in the field or in General Hospital #2.

In early February alarmingly high numbers of patients were admitted to Ward 2 and to the hospital with dysentery, malaria, and symptoms of starvation. No longer could I say that all the beds were full. Our orders were to put blankets on the ground and place patients on the blankets. From the beginning there were no sheets on my ward. Even had there been, there was no way of getting them laundered. The facilities of the laundry were more or less overwhelmed by the material they received from the surgical wards. We had one lister bag just outside the ward which served as our source of water for all purposes. Patients did not get bathed, because there was neither water nor personnel to do so.

The problem with the dysentery patients was great. Many of them were so weak that they could not travel the distance from their beds to the latrine without soiling themselves. The path was marked with liquid feces. I lived in great fear that a patient, due to weakness, might fall into the toilet pits. The corpsmen were kept busy trying to help patients to the toilets and keeping the deposits scooped off the ground. What medication we had was almost totally ineffectual in stopping dysentery. Captain Jack Comstock, who had the admitting ward, adopted the rule that no patient who could not make it to the toilet without soiling himself, the ground, or the bed could sleep on a mattress. At about the same time I put the same rule in effect on my ward. I hated to put such sick, weak men on the ground, but there was no escaping it. As the ward census grew by leaps and bounds, we were compelled to take the mattresses off the beds and use them for patients who did not have uncontrolled diarrhea.

By early March 1942 the supply of quinine had become totally inadequate even for the treatment of those with clinical malaria. None was available for prophylaxis. My own malaria was quiescent, so I took no quinine. In late February or early March we heard rumors that a huge supply of quinine was being flown in from Mindanao. Although I distrusted this rumor, as I had become accustomed to mistrust all rumors, a plane from Mindanao did arrive at Cabcaben airfield with 150,000 tablets of quinine. With at least 50,000 malarial patients on that little thumb of a peninsula, Bataan, this shipment provided treatment for less than one-half day.

One of the most remarkable things coming out of our experience in Bataan was the presence and performance of the army nurses. In retrospect I believe that they were the greatest morale boost present in tha unhappy little area of jungle called Bataan. I was continually amazed that anyone living and working under such primitive conditions could remain as calm, pleasant, efficient and impeccably neat and clean as these remarkable nurses. I believe that their presence in the wards around that sprawling hospital meant more to the patients than any other single thing.

Then, too, the aura of femininity extended beyond the confines of General Hospital #2. Some of the men in the combat area who had a moment of quietness in the battlefield would steal away to the hospital to spend a short while in the company of a woman. Often in the evening hours Jack and I would hear girlish giggles coming across the Real River from the burlap confines, accompanied by male voices speaking in low tones. They were generally very careful to keep from disturbing their fellow nurses who were trying to sleep. Jack and I, who slept nearer to the nurses' quarters than anyone else, never lost any sleep due to the male visitors across the Real. We were so tired at the end of the day that we drifted off almost immediately.

In my mind, however, and in the minds of others, there lurked the fear that we would be unable to protect the nurses should the Japanese combat troops overrun the hospital. We had all heard the stories out of China about the atrocities committed against the female population of Nanking. Even today, in spite of all the efforts to maintain that women properly belong in combat situations, I must admit that the thought of placing women in the front lines in a situation such as existed in Bataan offends me. There is something ingrained and inbred in man, though he may laugh at the idea, which persuades him that he is the protector.

As the war continued month after month, the population of my ward and the rest of the hospital increased dramatically. After the second week in March the inflow of starved, exhausted, very ill men was overwhelming. Making ward rounds was almost a futile task for me, Lieutenant A.N. Sarwald, and Lieutenant Oberst. Dirty, unshaven, and hollow-eyed, the incoming patients now all showed marked signs of malnutrition in addition to their other ills. My ward, which was intended to hold 100 patients or fewer, grew to over 400. They lay on blankets, mattresses, or the ground itself. Half or more had lost their mosquito nets while fighting and retreating. At this time I too was suffering from malarial infection and was further weakened by a severe diarrhea. I was so weak that I could barely drag myself around, but comparatively speaking I was much better than most of my patients.

By early March, after prolonged dependence on a diet lacking the entire B spectrum, almost every patient arriving at General Hospital #2 showed some signs of deficiency diseases. In many cases the milled rice, having been in storage for many months, had an added mixture of insects and rat manure. The only dairy products were tins of condensed milk, available for only the most ill patients. There were occasional servings of a stew laced with carabao and mule meat. A few times during March patients were served canned fruit, cracked wheat, and insect infested oatmeal. After mid–March coffee and tea were no longer available. A great effort was made during march to give the very seriously ill as much of the more nourishing food as possible, but the increased efforts to supply more of these food items to the sicker men were met with a waning supply. By April 1, 1942, the fruit juices, canned milk, and meat were gone. From then until the surrender on April 10 our diet was almost exclusively milled rice.

War Plan Orange called for an armed force of about 30,000 men to retreat into Bataan. All civilians were to be evacuated. In actuality, about 80,000 troops and 26,000 civilians were on the peninsula. This was more than triple the number planned for, resulting in nearly 120,000 people being fed with only one-third the amount of food needed. In addition, to compound the problem, those 30,000 civilians had to depend on the army for medical treatment. This meant that there were about 120,000 persons, civilian and military, compressed onto this small bit of territory – 120,000 miserable, starved, malaria-infected persons, who were trapped like animals. Never before in our history had American forces been forced into such a pocket of misery.

On the day before Easter Sunday we were told that we would be served steaks for our midday meal on Easter. I think that for purposes of morale, and because everyone seemed to sense that the end was near, a maximum effort was made to exhaust all sources in order to make that one day memorable. We were dressed in our best uniforms, and the nurses looked their prettiest. We enjoyed what was to be our last good meal for a long time. Later we learned that our steaks were from the last of the fabled 26th Cavalry. I believe that the steeds of the 26th could not in their demise have served a more noble purpose.

In early April 1942 the conditions at General Hospital #2 deteriorated at a much accelerated pace, with the situation on the front line rapidly worsening as well. A Japanese attack had caused a breakthrough at Mount Samat and the clearing stations near the front lines were filled with thousands of patients. The general hospitals were already filled to overflowing, so that it was practically impossible to transfer those in the clearing stations. We feared, however, that if the front were overrun by the Japanese and the clearing stations invaded, the sick in those stations might be slaughtered. The patients therefore were moved into General Hospital #2, where the census was nearly 4,000 on April 1, roughly 6,000 on April 8, and finally 7,000 on April 10, the day of surrender. At that time General Hospital #2 was said to be the largest army hospital in the history of our country. To accommodate so many sick patients – feed them, give adequate medication, and keep records – was an impossible task with the available personnel and supplies. Our situation was chaotic. We were trying to take care of 7,000 men who had been unrelieved at the front for the past three months. During those three months they had been on starvation rations, and the majority, to add to their debilitation, suffered from malaria and or dysentery.

The picture in General Hospital #2 was almost indescribable. In the last few days before surrender it was more a temporary haven than a hospital. Along with the human misery was the constant din of artillery fire. The guns of the Japanese fired over our heads at Corregidor, and the guns of Corregidor fired back over our heads at the Japanese. After late January the front line ran across the narrow waist of Bataan extending from Pilar to Bagac. This line at the narrowest point was approximately ten miles across. At Pilar the Japanese front was seven and a half to eight miles north of General Hospital #2. We could see the flashes of the guns on the front, and then a few seconds later hear the roar as some of the shells from Corregidor went over our heads. The ungodly screeching noise was bad enough in the daytime but very disturbing at night. Considerable shrapnel landed in the hospital area, and we were requested to wear helmets. A few shells fell short, some landing in the graveyard and disinterring a few of the bodies. One shell landed in the main kitchen, killing a cook and injuring several others. The hospital, too, was a very hazardous combat area.

By the afternoon of April 7, 1942, the U.S. armed forces had retreated to a line extending from Limay on the east to the slopes of Mount Mariveles on the west and just south of the Mariveles River. This retreat placed General Hospital #2 just eight miles from the front lines of a rapidly deteriorating situation. After that critical date we were still receiving casualties from the front line and evacuees from the front line clearing stations. We were aware from April 7 that the end was imminent. News both official and unofficial came into the hospital that the fight for Bataan was nearly over. It was to be the greatest defeat ever suffered by United States forces in the field.

The end was so near that on the evening of April 8, just after nightfall, I was summoned to headquarters by Colonel Gillespie. When I walked into headquarters he was talking with Colonel Jack Schwartz and Colonel "Rhiney" Craig. "John," he said, "we've received word from General King that surrender is near and that we must, as soon as possible, evacuate the nurses to Corregidor." I was instructed to go with all haste and notify the nurses to assemble at headquarters with all the possessions they could get in one musette bag. The nurses very quickly got together a very few necessities and were ready to go. There was no hysteria, no panic, no unnecessary ado; they came very quietly. I was informed, however, that a few nurses remained on the surgical ward, and a few others were saying good-bye to boyfriends. The roundup did not take very long, though, and the nurses were placed in whatever conveyance could be found that had gasoline and would still run.

From General Hospital #2 to Mariveles was only three miles, but the general bedlam, congested traffic, stalled vehicles, thousands on foot moving to the rear, and the blowing up of an ammunition dump caused hours of delay. The nurses almost failed to get through. The barge to transport them to Corregidor left just before dawn, stranding them on the beach. Finally on the early morning of April 9 they were picked up by a lighter and taken to Corregidor. Soon after the nurses left the pier at Mariveles the whole area was blasted by Japanese bombers. All of the nurses made it safely to Corregidor.

With the evacuation of the nurses there settled an atmosphere of gloom across the hospital. It was as if the spirit of the place had departed. We had known that the time for us was running short, but with the nurses gone it seemed that what we had not fully accepted had now become an absolute. As Jack and I returned to our cots by the Real, for a while we were in an absolute silence. Then Jack gave me a real surprise. From the bottom of his duffel bag he pulled out a magnum of fine champagne: "John, I've been saving this for a victory celebration, but I guess that can't happen. It would be a damn shame for this good champagne to fall in the hands of the Japanese." We called over a couple of our closer friends and drank to the unknown.

It was a good thing that we did not know on that night what was ahead of us—the starvation, the disease, the confinement. For some unaccountable reason, perhaps the champagne, I slept well that night. However, when morning came and I had to deal with reality, I felt none of the exhilaration of the night before.

CHAPTER 8

Prisoners of the Japanese

April 9, 1942–June 1, 1942

The collapse of our front line at Cabcaben threw the region into chaos. Concerned primarily with the rounding up of the combat troops near Mariveles, the Japanese Army swept by General Hospital #2 as if it were not there. We medical officers and corpsmen still had the obligation to try to care for the 7,000 patients still at General Hospital #2. On the morning of April 9, 1942, we placed Red Cross signs and large white sheets in conspicuous places to identify the area as a hospital. The Japanese were still bombing and strafing nearby, and we were getting a large number of shell fragments in the hospital itself. In the midst of all the din and confusion we prepared to surrender the hospital.

A little after dark on the 10th all of the medical officers were summoned to the headquarters shack, where we found Colonel Gillespie and his adjutant, Major Clinton Maupin, seated at their desks surrounded by two very junior Japanese officers and several Japanese enlisted men. The Japanese had with them an interpreter who knew just enough English to get the message across. The more junior of the two Japanese officers read a number of rules which the personnel of the surrendered hospital were commanded to observe. After each rule was read in Japanese, the interpreter translated into his fractured English, concluding with a flourish: "Anyone caught violating this rule will be shooted." The two rules which I remember best concerned the Real River and our supplies. We would be shot if we were caught bathing in the Real River, and we would be shot if we were caught looting our own supplies. All American property was now to be considered the property of the Imperial Army. If I recall properly, the other items for which we could be "shooted" were failure to observe a blackout and straying off the confines of the hospital.

Guards were posted here and there in the hospital and signs were posted in Japanese. There were frequent visitations by Japanese officers, most of them carrying cameras. They seemed to enjoy promenading through the hospital, and at times they even paused in the middle of the hospital to rest. The Japanese enlisted men wandering through the hospital seemed to be more specifically interested in watches, rings, and food. And as they made their way through the hospital, they collected every such item which anyone was foolish enough to expose. In anticipation of such activity, Jack and I had given most of our valuables to a nurse to take with her to Corregidor. The most obnoxious trait of our captors was their habit, whenever nature called, of squatting in their tracks and relieving themselves.

Within 48 hours, the Japanese had looted all the remaining food we had carefully saved to ration out to the very sick. We were soon without our small supply of sardines, canned milk, and fruit juice. Colonel Gillespie protested this confiscation of our desperately needed food and medical suplies, but the Japanese medical officer to whom he protested, Major Sekeeguchi, made it clear that nothing should be held back if requested by the Japanese army. He further pronounced that any effort by our personnel to withhold such supplies would be severely punished. While discussing the matter with Colonel Gillespie, Major Sekeeguchi became irate, ordering that the subject not be brought up again. But Colonel Gillespie, not a man to give up, asked that signs be put up to request that food supplies, medical supplies, and personal possessions be off limits to Japanese soldiers. These signs were put up but proved totally ineffectual; the Japanese continued to roam freely and take whatever they wished. After the looting of our food supplies our diet was solely boiled rice – polished, cracked, weevilly, and loaded with rat feces. This diet was all we had so we ate it.

The second day after our surrender, the Japanese instructed all Filipinos to leave the hospital. Colonel Jack Schwartz, a compassionate and courageous man, tried very hard to persuade those men, all patients, that they should not leave, but he was not successful. They had been led to believe that they were now free, and they left, thousands of them. The majority were suffering from malaria, dysentery, malnutrition, and wounds. Once they reached the highway they were forced to join the thousands of other Filipinos and Americans on the Death March out of Bataan. These Filipino soldiers were in general sick, without food, and without water. On their way out of Bataan, 800 died from thirst, starvation, disease, and atrocities committed by the Japanese. The exodus of the Filipinos left about 1,500 American military personnel as patients at General Hospital #2.

A few days before our surrender, a pregnant Filipino woman had wandered into our hospital obviously near term and in labor. She was delivered in the OR and put to bed in a small tent on one of the medical wards. She was so weak and sick after delivery that no one had the heart to send her away at the time of surrender. The commanding officer of the hospital made every effort possible to keep her presence unknown to the Japanese, who wandered everywhere in the hospital, but the baby's cries brought her to the attention of the Japanese, who raped her repeatedly at gunpoint. It would have been foolhardy for anyone to have tried to protect her. I am quite sure that any officer or enlisted man trying to intervene would have been shot summarily. The poor baby was thin, sickly, and feverish. The doctor on the ward suspected malaria and asked Captain Harold W. Keschner, our pathologist, to do blood smears. To the pathologist's great surprise he found the infant's blood teeming with microfilaria (indicating the condition known as filariasis) which he identified immediately as a parasite transmitted by several species of mosquitoes. Fortunately the patient infected with filariasis usually recovers. I have no idea about the ultimate fate of the mother and infant, and since the chance that their story ended happily is low, I cannot say that I wish to know.

After all the Filipinos were gone, we tried to consolidate the remaining patients into a more central area. My ward was located nearest the highway, so it was consolidated with another one near headquarters.

Soon after the surrender, our hospital was completely encircled by Japanese artillery aimed at Corregidor, and the guns on Corregidor were aimed at the Japanese ringed about us. We were truly in a combat zone. I do not believe that any other American army hospital has ever been in such a precarious setting. Firing from the Japanese toward Corregidor continued intermittently day and night. Jack Comstock's receiving ward was struck by the nose of a 14-inch shell, and several patients were killed. There were plenty of foxholes and trenches in which to seek refuge, but staying in a foxhole day and night was a lot of trouble. Most of us preferred to wear our helmets and take a chance. We received many shell fragments from both Japanese and Corregidor guns. On April 22 some shells landed in a ward and in the mess hall. Around 20 personnel and patients were killed and injured. On several occasions duds landed in the hospital, fortunately injuring no one. Protests to the Japanese by our commanding officer were of no avail. Colonel Gillespie wished the patients moved to a safer place, but the Japanese officer's answer was that until the fortress of Corregidor surrendered there would be no removal of patients or personnel.

Colonel Gillespie felt that since American troops at Corregidor knew exactly where we were, the artillery would try to avoid dropping shells into the hospital. Colonel Gillespie thought also that the Japanese viewed the hospital and its near surroundings as providing a relative haven from the shells fired from Corregidor. By the afternoon of May 6 we sensed that Corregidor had fallen, though the Japanese continued the rain of artillery shells on that small island until that evening. On May 4 alone some 16,000 shells fell on the tiny island.

Soon after the surrender of Corregidor Colonel Gillespie was ordered to remove all seriously ill patients to General Hospital #1. The transfer was made in those several buses which had been converted earlier to sleeping quarters for the nurses. The fact that the buses had been fueled by gasoline was kept concealed from the Japanese Army.

Sufficient gas had been kept hidden for just such an emergency. About 600 of the most seriously ill were removed to General Hospital #1 on May 11. Colonel Gillespie had the courage and foresight to transfer, in addition to patients, a small supply of medications which were desperately needed for their care. He did this with neither the knowledge nor consent of Major Sekeeguchi, who had previously ordered that no medical supplies should be removed from General Hospital #2. We felt that Colonel Gillespie's courage at that time was instrumental in saving hundreds of lives. The remaining patients at General Hospital #2, numbering some 700, were moved first to Bilibid prison in Manila and then to Cabanatuan POW camp. The medical personnel of General Hospital #2 were transferred to the vicinity of General Hospital #1. At the time of transfer many of the officers and enlisted men were quite ill from malaria and dysentery. I was weak from my untreated malaria and had a bad case of dysentery, but Jack took great care of me. He was able to scrounge a few quinine pills, enough to end the chills and fever. He was also able to find a unit of plasma which was given to me, and after quinine and plasma I felt much better, though our diets still consisted of cracked, moldy rice laced with rat droppings.

Jack, for some reason, knew quite a bit about the surrounding area, and after I perked up a bit, he told me that just across the main north-south highway was a quartermaster depot he felt we should explore. He was hoping that the Japanese had overlooked a few items when they looted the area. I was reluctant, but Jack was persuasive. I didn't like the prominent signs displayed in the area which warned that leaving the boundaries set for us and looting were both offenses punishable by death. We approached the highway with utmost care because vehicles loaded with Japanese military frequently passed in both directions. From where we stood we could see what appeared to be a Filipino army uniform and a pair of shoes lying in the middle of the highway. As we darted across the road we saw near the uniform a human head flattened across the road. Even in my haste I had to pause, if only momentarily. The face, a grinning, grotesque mask, was spread out to an absolute smoothness, having been run over repeatedly. In the few seconds we lingered in horror, it struck me that war dehumanized both victor and victim. East of the highway and a mile or two from the bay were several deserted quartermaster bodegas. Each building was plastered with signs warning of the death penalty for looting. We explored several buildings, finding nothing but army shoes, but finally we found a large underground cavelike structure which the quartermaster corps had used for shelter during the heavy bombing and artillery fire. Apparently many men of the quartermaster corps had slept there; bedding was on the floor and clothes hung on the wall. I saw nothing usable, but Jack had great persistence. He ferreted out two or three small caches of food that had been stowed away. Our trove was two cans of salmon, three cans of sardines, and two cans of baked beans. You would have believed from our expressions of delight that we had uncovered an entire food mart. When we got to the highway, we paused in a grove of trees until the highway was clear in both directions; and then we sped across the highway into more trees. Colonel Craig and Colonel Gillespie were happy to see us get back; both had considered our foray risky.

Jack, however, was not satisfied; he wanted next to go back after the shoes. I was not at my best physically, and the trip of the day before had worn me down still further. I still had diarrhea, and my weight was down to 116 pounds. Since I declared myself incapacitated, Jack asked Major Bob Lewis to go along with him. They did go, using the same route and the same precautions as the day before. They found the shoes and loaded up with a few dozen pairs of army-issue boots. However, on the way back to our area they suddenly ran into a Japanese patrol of three soldiers. The Japanese were in a jovial mood and made some gestures to indicate that Americans were big-footed but not very smart. After a short delay the Japanese motioned Jack and Bob on their way. Jack opined that these Japanese were different from those which we had seen previously. Jack and Bob could just as easily have run into some Japanese who would have shot them on sight for looting. From that little sortie Jack and Bob supplied several members of the group with an extra pair of boots. On May 25 the Japanese informed us that on the next day we would be leaving.

On May 26 we were all crowded into a few trucks for the ride over a rough dusty highway. None of us had the faintest idea where we were being taken. We were stunned when we arrived in Manila the next day and were marched into a grim fortress-like place called Bilibid Prison. I had heard something of the history of Bilibid Prison, where political prisoners under Spanish and later American rule were held. The prison had dungeons where some Filipino insurgents such as Aguinaldo, the leader of the Filipino insurrection, had been chained.

We arrived at Bilibid on May 26 after dark, and were marched at a double-quick pace through the gates. The Japanese at this time employed a technique with which I was to become much more familiar as time went on. The idea seemed to be if they yelled, shouted, screamed, shoved, prodded, and hit, we would become totally intimidated. They really need not have bothered; I was already totally intimidated. I was also dirty, exhausted, and depressed.

After the clamor and confusion of our arrival, we were hustled across the compound, up some worn stone steps, and into a large room which we were told was to be our quarters. The room was totally without furnishings, the floor was bare concrete, and there was only space to sit or lie down. Some of the officers, the old army hands, majors, and colonels, had brought footlockers with them; but as soon as they arrived the footlockers were confiscated by the Japanese. They were allowed to keep their toilet articles, their razors, their toothbrushes, and a change of clothes. I never had anything the Japanese wanted, so I was never looted. The windows to our quarters were not glassed in, which was fortunate since it was terribly hot. Bulbs too dim to read by hung from the ceiling. It was hard to understand why, but they were kept burning all night. The air was full of mosquitoes, and there was absolutely no place to hang our mosquito nets. If one draped the net over his face, those bloodthirsty insects would just drink their fill of blood through the netting. Jack and I learned clever ways to drape the net over our bodies and dispose part of the netting so that it stayed away from our faces.

That first night, just after midnight, we were given a serving of boiled rice. I had lost nearly all the fat from an always lean tailbone, and sleeping on that concrete with only a blanket under me was a miserable experience. To add to our discontent the Japanese guards were allowed to roam at will among us looking for watches and rings. They would shake us, shine a light in our faces, and look for loot. They were always disappointed when they searched my belongings.

By the next morning Jack and I both had a very sore rear and sore back. Jack had experienced more difficulty than I; his hip and ankle were so sore he could hardly walk. Our diet at Bilibid continued to be, purely and simply, rice and more rice. On May 29 Colonel Gillespie moved around among us and related that our group of doctors, dentists, and medical corpsmen would be moved soon to form a hospital to treat sick POWS. He had not been informed where we were going. Our stay at Bilibid was far from pleasant. Even though the outer walls were rather distant from our quarters, there was always the feeling of being pent up.

On May 30 we were awakened very early, 1 or 2 A.M., fed our rice a little before dawn, and marched out of Bilibid prison. It was not fully day as we marched through the streets of Manila. Surprisingly, in spite of the hour there were many Filipinos, silent and undemonstrative, who lined the streets to see us paraded past. The march was to the railway station where we were loaded on some small freight cars that seemed to be designed for horses or cattle. The Japanese crammed 90 into each car, forcing us so close that we had to stand. The floors were covered with straw interlaced with manure. After they closed the door on us, the heat and the stench became almost intolerable. We rode about six hours in the horsecars, and I remember that we were given water and some fruit once on the way. From the railway station in the little town of Cabanatuan we were marched to a schoolyard surrounded by a barbed wire fence.

Apparently the enclosure had been used before to hold prisoners. There were no latrines, and the ground was littered with both animal and human excrement. There was one single pit in the corner of the compound which was full of maggots and liquid feces. We had just arrived inside the fence when the Japanese began wandering among us looking for loot, but most of our watches and rings were gone. At about sundown the Japanese drove up with a large iron cauldron, some water, and a bag of rice. We had boiled rice and unsweetened tea for our evening meal. When it began to rain, Jack and I crawled under the schoolhouse to keep dry but discovered that the ground under the building was covered with chicken and dog excrement. We scooped away enough of the filth to put down a folded blanket and tried to sleep, but no sleep came.

At 11:00 or 12:00 that evening the night was penetrated with a loud voice which repeated over and over, "There is no war, there is no war." It was as if some soul had found the war too horrible to contemplate and his subconscious was denying its existence. The voice was so loud and so penetrating on an otherwise silent night that I became afraid the Japanese might do violence to him. I got out from under the building and walked to the area where some men were trying to silence the voice, and as I neared I saw that the man crying into the night was James Marshall. He had not lost his sanity during his horrible experiences in the Spanish Civil War, but the cumulative effect of that war and what he had seen in the present one caused him to snap. We finally persuaded Jim to cease his cry, and the night became still, except for the sound of cicadas, whose shrill cry continued.

On the last day of May we were aroused before sunup, fed soupy rice and marched in formation out of that appalling place. Marching east through the countryside away from that little town of Cabanatuan, we had walked about 16 kilometers by late morning. It was extremely hot, and our packs grew heavier as we went. Some became so burdened that they threw away part of their load; others collapsed and had to be placed on a Japanese truck tailing us.

When we finally got to what was called Camp #1, I was totally exhausted and much in need of water, but Camp #1 had no water so we had to wait several hours for water to be brought from Camp #2. We each had about four ounces of incredibly thin rice gruel for our supper. We were quartered in old abandoned Filipino army barracks meant to shelter about 40, but the Japanese managed to cram at least 100 men into such limited space. On June 1 we were awakened by the Japanese and given a meal of very thin soup and boiled rice. I don't know why they counted us so often, unless they didn't trust their arithmetic, but we were counted and recounted several times that morning. I remember the date, June 1, very clearly since I had laboriously carved it on the lid of my mess kit. There had been a considerable amount of rain the night before, so we were able to catch enough for drinking, washing our faces, and shaving.

Soon after the noon hour we were ordered to get ready for another hike, nearly nine kilometers this time. Jack held sick call among the men and found out that many could not make the hike. The weaker ones were put on a truck to be carried to Camp #2, hereafter called Cabanatuan. Jack himself had a very tough time making it to Camp #2. He was totally exhausted.

The new camp left much to be desired. It was the rainy season and the ground was an ooze of mud. The buildings were the same as those at Camp #1 – Filipino army barracks of nipa, bamboo, sawali, and cogon grass. There were no doors; the barracks were open ended, and on a windy day it was like living in a wind tunnel. Down the center of the building ran a split bamboo floor; and on either side running the length of the structure were two tiers divided into five bays (for a total of 20 bays). The roofs were of nipa palm, and the walls were made of sawali (woven bamboo strips). The Japanese put 108 men in my particular barracks, and it was very, very crowded.

The latrines were a dismal mess. They were pit privies, very similar to the backwoods' three or four holer. Those pits were practically full of water, due to the rain. Overlaying the contents of those pits was a teeming mass of water, feces, and maggots. One dreaded to make the trip of 200 to 300 yards, even with an urgent call of nature. Each time one walked to the latrine he picked up considerably sticky, gummy mud on his shoes, and shortly the bamboo walkway between the sleeping spaces was covered with mud which we had no way of removing. We were tired, hungry, and miserable, and our feelings were not helped by having to wait until near midnight for our rice. In spite of the bleak surroundings, I found the bamboo to be softer than the concrete floor at Bilibid and I slept well the night of June 1.

CHAPTER 9

Cabanatuan I

June 1942

I had thought that our own raggle-taggle, starved crew from
General Hospital #2 was the endpoint of human misery, but the second day after we arrived at Cabanatuan, I changed my mind. Seven
hundred men, or shadows of men, walked into Cabanatuan from the
railway station where they had arrived by train in cattle cars from
Camp O'Donnell. These tired, sick, emaciated specters were lined up
to be counted by the Japanese. Most of them were in shorts, many
nude to their waists. They had pitifully few belongings, since they had
long since been looted by the Japanese. Most of them, for unexplained
reasons, were deeply tanned. Their ribs, which showed deeply sunken
grooves between, were starkly outlined against their chests. Practically all subcutaneous fat was gone. Their legs and arms looked like

pipestems. That June we would receive several shipments of such dehumanized cargo from Camp O'Donnell.

These men were some of the survivors of the infamous Bataan Death March. The Japanese, expecting to transport about 25,000 prisoners to the camps being prepared on Luzon, were unable to handle the nearly three times that number captured. With too few truck and rail transports available, most of the men had to walk. Even worse, the Japanese, expecting the captured allies to have their own rations, had far too little food to decently feed the prisoners. The already starving, sick, and exhausted men had to slog some 65 miles over jungle trails. Most of the Japanese guards exhibited unforgivable brutality along the way. Herded at bayonet point, the prisoners of war were driven almost beyond human endurance. Stragglers were clubbed mercilessly, while the sick and starving were abandoned to die. Many of the dying were buried alive by their own comrades at gunpoint. The Filipinos were treated especially badly; at one point nearly 300 were bayonetted.

Although no one knows the exact numbers, about 9,300 Americans and 45,000 Filipinos survived the march and made it to the camps. About 25,000 succumbed along the way to wounds, disease, or brutal mistreatment. Denied adequate food and medicine by their Japanese captors, thousands more men would die needlessly in the camps.

The camp at Cabanatuan was quickly divided into two areas, one of which was farcically called a hospital. The hospital only served to segregate the very ill from the less ill. Of course, there had been absolutely no preparation to care for the sick. Thousands of prisoners were very ill with malaria, and there was no quinine to treat them. At least as many were suffering from dysentery, which was further depleting their already malnourished bodies. Without exception the prisoners were suffering from malnutrition and vitamin deficiency. Many of the troops, especially those that had been at O'Donnell, had ulcers and blisters on their feet caused by walking in ill-fitting shoes and by poor sanitation.

Jack and I were assigned wards in this "hospital," which had a population that at times rose as high as 3,000 and averaged about 2,500 to 2,600. It was startling to find that among those put in the hospital, and indeed those not put in the hospital, hundreds had swelling of their feet and ankles largely due to diets deficient in protein.

We saw hundreds of cases which would be classed as wet beri-beri, though we could not be certain of the precise cause of the edema. In our situation, we rarely dealt with a pure complex of any one disease; almost always it was a spectrum of various diseases. Observation proved that we were dealing with a dependent edema. At times when the patient had been lying down for several hours at night his facial features would be almost obliterated by swelling, but after he sat or stood the edema would migrate to his feet, ankles, and legs. If he sat all day some of the dropsy went to his buttocks. When we were able to give one of the edematous patients a significant feeding of animal protein, he would lose a lot of fluid through his urinary tract, and the edema would partly or completely go away, at least temporarily.

I often had as many as 120 patients on my ward, #29 (of 31). But since I had nothing with which to treat them, I felt less like a doctor than a caretaker of the dying. Our efforts were a travesty.

The officers assigned to the hospital were billeted in wooden buildings with floor space of about 14 by 18 feet. These structures had one large opening on each side which in rainy weather could be closed by a large shutter hinged to the side of the building. Fifteen of us shared a building, so there was no space to stow anything. We slept on the floor and put our meager belongings at the head of the pallet, a folded blanket. Later "Sammy," Captain Samuel Bloom, managed to find some tarpaulin and swung himself a hammock. There were no lights, and we had long since been relieved of any flashlights we might have had. After sundown there was nothing to do but go to bed, lie there and tell tall tales. We did have a great deal of difficulty putting up our mosquito nets, since there was no way to hang them up in the usual way. We compromised by attaching one end of the net to the wall above our heads and draping the rest of it over our lower bodies and feet. In retrospect it is amazing that we were able to remain friends, living in such cramped quarters.

More and more of the starved, emaciated, wraith-like individuals continued to arrive from O'Donnell, and without exception they were suffering from not one but a number of ills. Those shadows of men had been in Bataan and on the Death March. Their treatment at O'Donnell can only be described as bestial; they were tortured, starved, and grossly maltreated – and 1,500 died.

After their suffering at O'Donnell and on Bataan, these men walked from the train station to the Cabanatuan prisoner of war

Exterior and interior views of Ward 29 (the hospital) at Cabanatuan.

camp. Hundreds of them were barefoot, their tattered clothes filthy and ragged. Those left were indeed survivors, but from their appearance and the seemingly hopeless situation at Cabanatuan I had great doubt that many of those pitiful scarecrows could long continue to survive. I saw man after man walk into Cabanatuan clasping only a burlap bag around his body.

At Cabanatuan, in addition to the shortage of water for bathing, we had no soap or toilet paper. The men could only try to cleanse their mess gear by wiping it with a tuft of grass. All of these elements plus the filth, the flies, and debilitation served to augment the terrible epidemic of dysentery. After the first week the hospital was realigned in an attempt to segregate the dysentery patients. The situation reminded me of Ward 2 at General Hospital #2. The majority of those men had very frequent, very loose, watery stools, with no control. A good portion of them could not stand up, much less walk to a toilet 100 yards distant, so they soiled themselves repeatedly. A good percentage could stagger outside the building and make an attempt to reach the toilet, only to fail; consequently the ground was strewn with liquid feces covered with flies. However, the worst humiliation came to those who slept on a bay below a patient with uncontrolled dysentery. The person in the lower bay could awake to find himself covered with liquid feces that had dripped down between the bamboo strips. We tried very hard to keep the sicker men on the lower bays, but there was no predicting when a moderately ill man would suddenly reach the uncontrolled state.

Many of the men on the non-hospital side of Cabanatuan were just as ill as those in the hospital, but having heard about the conditions in the "hospital" they vigorously resisted relocation. Some actually had to be in extremis, almost terminally ill, before they were moved to a barracks-ward.

I had recurrent episodes of malarial chills and fever which were kept, most of the time, at a subclinical level. Jack was a very resourceful person; by one means or another, he managed to scrounge enough quinine pills to subdue the parasites temporarily. I also had a recurrent problem with diarrhea, but it only got me off of my feet for a few days at a time.

Along with his scrounging, Jack was also a great purveyor of optimistic rumors: we would get medicines; the Allies were achieving victories. He wanted so badly to believe such stories that he actually did. I resisted, though. I had a great fear of the letdown which usually followed these floating fantasies called news.

One very tantalizing thing which we were able to observe was the presence of friendly Filipinos who brought food and medicine within a few hundred feet of the compound fence. They meant to sell or give us the bananas, the mangoes, and the eggs, but the Japanese guards would drive them away before they could make contact. Sometimes they came at night, and with great daring, sold and bartered through the less well-guarded places along the fence.

Our problems were compounded by lack of water. We had a few taps from which to refill our canteens, but the supply was not adequate to permit us to bathe or wash clothes. My blankets and my clothes had not been washed since the surrender. On the sixth or seventh day after our arrival at Cabanatuan we had a heavy rain, and everyone who was able stood outside nude and looked appreciatively toward heaven. It was a zany sight to see all those skinny men running around splashing water over themselves. As the days passed, it seemed that with the absence of medicine and the presence of a starvation diet our situation would only get worse.

In the rainy season, everywhere we walked was sticky, gummy mud. Our camp area had been a rice paddy before being taken over by the Filipino army. About 40 percent of the hospital area was low lying, and consequently during the rainy season it was a morass. Our shoes, which we had been so careful to keep, were of no use. As soon as the young artisans in the hospital could supply them, our shoes were replaced with clogs, or getas. At Cabanatuan, as everywhere else, resourceful ones supplied our needs. The getas were simply a piece of hardwood carved to the shape of the foot with an added strap to hold the clog in place. The wood was largely purloined from the kitchens, where it was stored for cooking. The straps came from any place the clog maker could find a piece of canvas, thick cloth, or blanket. During the rainy seasons, regular shoes remained damp and moldy, never free of the sticky mud. The clogs, on the other hand, were easy to clean.

The same conditions continued at Cabanatuan until about the first of July 1942. Of the over 6,000 POWs at Cabanatuan at that time, approximately half were in the hospital. The Japanese provided no medicine or nourishing food. And except for the trickle that came in through the fence, we were totally without quinine.

One area in which the Japanese were exceedingly thorough was bango, or roll call. There would be a mix-up from time to time, and patients who were quite ill would at times wander to another ward. If they were not present for roll call, we would be kept in place till the count was completed. There was much frantic scurrying around in an effort to return all of our charges to their proper places. The Japanese were not really concerned about the condition of those bodies – dead or alive – but the count had to be accurate.

Some of us in our crowded quarters had tried to make ourselves more comfortable. Jack, the ever resourceful, had managed to create a bunk that raised him two feet off the ground. Others in our bahay were equally clever in making their beds more comfortable. However, the Japanese in a surprise inspection of our quarters declared that we must tear out the bunks and sleep on the floor. Jack was most unhappy because his hip could not tolerate the hard floor. The Japanese had barely gotten out of sight when "Sammy" Bloom restrung his hammock.

A few days before the Japanese had kicked down our beds, I myself had had a very ludicrous experience. My rear, always skinny, but much more so now that I had lost so much weight, also did not tolerate the hard boards very well. To get some padding for my bed, I set out from our bahay toward the western part of the hospital compound where there was a patch of cogon grass. Unfortunately the cogon grass was near the fence and in plain sight of the Nipponese guardhouse. I had barely reached the plot when I heard a loud uproar; Japanese soldiers, armed with rifles, came boiling out of the guardhouse, running towards me. At that moment I felt that I was in real trouble, and when they came toward me jabbering Japanese and presenting bayonets, I was ill at ease, especially when they started marching me toward the guardhouse, prodding me with their bayonets (ironically in the rear) with every step.

The hospital headquarters was only about 100 yards from the Japanese guardhouse. When Major Clinton Maupin and Lieutenant Henry Sechrest heard the alarm, they came running. By gestures and signs they conveyed to the Japanese that I was merely in search of bedding. The few tufts of cogon grass in my hands bore proof that I was indeed not trying to escape. One of the Japanese guards yanked the grass out of my hands and gestured for me to be gone. As we walked back to the hospital headquarters, Major Maupin admonished me: "John, you nut, do you want to get yourself killed?" I was totally chastened – and lucky. Some of the prisoners who wandered too near the fence were shot at from the guard tower, and some were killed.

Death from a bullet would have been preferable to the desolate and hopeless circumstances which overcame hundreds of others. I could have easily predicted the rise of the death rate in view of the deficient diet and the lack of medication. For the first week or ten days at Cabanatuan there were about ten deaths per day. By the middle of June the grisly procession of dead had grown alarmingly to

average 20 deaths per day – 20 men who had endured the terrible
ordeal of Bataan, who were 10,000 miles from home, and who then
died in the most miserable circumstances. For me, as a doctor, the
most distressing thought was that they could have been saved, almost
without exception, by proper diet and medical care.

Soon after the middle of June 1942 we were having as many as
30 deaths per day. I began to lose hope that any one of us in Cabanatuan would survive the war.

CHAPTER 10

Cabanatuan II

July 1942–December 1942

Toward the first of July 1942 we had yet another fear attached to our ever increasing list. Several cases of diphtheria appeared in camp. The diagnosis of diphtheria was easy: Captain Harold Keschner, our pathologist, could identify the organism by making smears of open lesions. Our problem was in treatment and isolation. Diphtheria is spread through droplets, spray of coughing, and direct contact with open lesions, and our men were crowded four to a bay intended for one man. All we could do was order that they sleep alternating head to foot and move the diphtheria patients to a separate ward. With no serum available for treatment, any severe infection such as diphtheria added to a weakened emaciated body is almost always lethal.

The first cases of diphtheria were diagnosed about the middle of June; over 100 men died, and the total number of cases rose to between 400 and 450. These deaths could be directly attributed to the wanton, deliberate neglect by the Japanese. After continuing pleas from Colonel "Rhiney" Craig and Colonel Jack Schwartz, we were able to get the idea across that the situation was dangerous for everyone, including the Japanese. After about ten weeks the hospital was supplied with enough antitoxin to treat a very few patients adequately, though the doctor in charge of treating the diphtheria patients, Captain Elack Schultz, instead used a much smaller dose in treating a larger number of patients. Captain Schultz did a splendid job with what he had to work with.

The nature of the patient population—men who were already ill from malaria, dysentery, and malnutrition—did not allow the disease to present in the usual way. The diphtheritic membrane occurred everywhere there was a mucous membrane—nose, throat, penis, rectum, urethra, tongue, and conjunctiva of the eye. Also frequently in the presence of open skin lesions the diphtheria would take root. But because of filthy conditions resulting from the lack of water (that first month was practically without rain) for washing bodies and clothes, there were many skin infections resembling impetigo present. The open skin lesions provided a ready portal for entry of the diphtheria bacillus.

The sanitation in the camp continued to be a tremendous problem. During the second and third months some effort was made to improve this problem, but we received little help from the Japanese. I recall vividly that in the very bad months the flies were a terrific problem. They were so numerous, and so ever-present, that there was a constant drone in the air. The barbed wire fence around the hospital stayed so thick with flies that the strands of wire looked like black rope. During the first several months we had to depend on rainwater for bathing and washing clothes. The patients, especially those with uncontrollable dysentery, were caked with filth. Those who were mobile could, when it rained, get out under the sky to bathe, but the very weak were compelled by their condition to lie in their own filth.

Even in the midst of all the squalor, some men seemed particularly pathetic and evocative of sympathy. One of these we called the "Yard-Bird." I never heard him called by any other name. He was on Jack Comstock's ward and came frequently under my observation.

How such things happen no one can be sure, but this American soldier was a 14-year-old child, just a few years older than a Little Leaguer; he was a school dropout, caught in the clutches of war. Every unit of any size had its Yard-Bird. The Yard-Bird, who never seemed to resent the title, had had such a great reservoir of discontent against his home or his school that he sought a way out. He lied about his age, as many others did, to get into the army. But any recruiter should have seen that he was only a child.

Our Yard-Bird had been in Bataan, on the Death March, at Camp O'Donnell, and finally in the prison camp at Cabanatuan. On that odyssey he had become bereft of all except some khaki shorts. He was hospitalized from a combination of malaria and dysentery. He had become a sort of mascot, and in a world where there was little to share other than kindness, there were many who in small ways came to his aid. The last and most enduring image I have of Yard-Bird came on a rainy evening on July 1942. He was standing in the mud and rain bare-headed, his blond hair plastered to his scalp, wearing an old Army overcoat which reached almost to his ankles, his feet shod in getas. He stood stock still, gazing into the distance as if he were trying to get a glimpse of home.

Of the numerous chaplains at Cabanatuan, I came to know one much better than the others – Chaplain Robert Preston Taylor, a devout, humble, and courageous man. Chaplain Taylor was tall, thin, red-haired, and freckled-faced. He, too, had come to the Philippines under the illusion that he would serve a year and then return to his wife in Texas. Assigned to the 31st Infantry, he had arrived in the Philippines in May 1941 and had not been allowed to bring his family.

Arriving in camp two to three weeks later than the medical personnel from General Hospital #2, Chaplain Taylor, along with Chaplain Oliver, the chief of chaplains in the Philippines, was greatly disturbed to learn the Japanese had forbidden any assembly for religious services; not even burial services for the dead were allowed at a time when men were dying some days at the rate of 60 to 70 per day. Even though he was not supposed to do so, Taylor insisted on accompanying the burial detail to the graveyard. At the graveside, against orders, Taylor knelt and said a prayer for the dead. The chaplains, Taylor included, had secret services and continued to comfort and counsel the sick and to perform last rites for the dying. Chaplain Taylor, I was told by his comrades, had also done heroic

Zero Ward: zero food, zero medicine, zero hope.

service with the 31st Infantry on Bataan, defying the Japanese on the Death March by intervening when Japanese soldiers were committing acts of brutality.

Equalling his courage were Chaplain Taylor's humility and deep spirituality. For that reason, among his assignments was the Zero Ward. With so many men dying during the summer months of July and August, we created the Zero Ward: a place of zero medicine, near zero supplies, and zero hope. It was where we doctors sent men to die. The majority selected for this pre-mortuary ward were dying of dysentery and lay in pools of their own filth. The building selected for use as the Zero Ward at the lower end of the compound was a long wooden building with no furnishings; Jack was the attending physician. The patients lay on the floor with only a blanket to cover them. There was one cold water tap at the front of this grisly ward, and during the day when the sun was shining and the weather was warm these men would be carried out, laid on the grass, and literally hosed down to remove the filth. They were without exception only ghosts of men. After the war, the pictures of the stacked bodies of the internees at Buchenwald reminded me of the Zero Ward at Cabanatuan. Chaplain Taylor was there to offer spiritual solace.

I recall one scene at that wretched spot which I am not allowed to forget. Just outside the Zero Ward two men near death had been hosed down and were lying on the ground in the warm sunshine. At that moment a visitor to the ward threw a cigarette butt to the ground between them. Both men, so feebly they could barely move, grabbed for the cigarette butt and with as much strength as they could summon in those ravaged bodies fought over it, half-crazed, like animals. Instead of returning immediately to my ward I walked over to speak to Captain Schultz on the diphtheria ward, and as I came back by a few minutes later I found the two men lying on the ground dead, the shredded cigarette butt on the ground between them.

Chaplain Taylor was even an accomplished barber, and managed to acquire some barbering tools. It was his feeling that we scruffy-looking characters needed an occasional haircut. Chaplain Taylor regularly cut my hair for me and in the process uplifted both my spiritual self and my morale. I believe few in the military can claim to have had their hair cut by a man who later became a major general and air force chief of chaplains.

Chaplain Taylor bravely aided his fellow prisoners and resisted the Japanese in any way he could. Actively engaged in the underground work, he was instrumental in getting considerable quinine and sulfa drugs brought into the camp by work details. Unfortunately, much of the medication was poorly labeled or carried names unfamiliar to us. We carefully experimented to determine how these drugs should be used.

During the summer of 1942 one of the work details had the audacity to sneak a shortwave radio into the camp, part by part. This radio was then used to contact the guerrillas in the eastern mountains of Luzon. Taylor let it be known through the radio channel that he wanted a Greek bible; soon thereafter a female courier was apprehended along with a shipment of medicine and a number of written messages to the prisoners at Cabanatuan. The Japanese traced the request for the bible to the chaplain, and Taylor, along with 12 other men whose names were detected in the correspondence, was arrested.

The chaplain was subjected to the most inhumane treatment in an effort to drag a confession out of him. He was placed in a 5 by 5 foot hot box with a half-crazed man who had been there for some time. The two had only a blanket for bedding and without netting were attacked

by clouds of mosquitoes. Day after day the chaplain remained in that place with the sun beating down on the metal roof. Their excrement lay around them. Their food, unfit for an animal, was limited. Preston Taylor spent many weeks in that hellhole until rather miraculously, through the intervention of Colonel William North and Colonel Jack Schwartz, the Japanese allowed him to be taken to the hospital. The real miracle was that Captain Taylor survived.

Another man in our group, Sergeant Thomas E. Hunt, a patient from my ward, #29, did not have the same good fortune. When Sergeant Hunt could no longer bear our plight, he disappeared through the fence one night in late June. At bango the next morning the Japanese really raised hell. They cared not whether we were fed or received proper medical treatment; their only concern was that, dead or alive, we be properly counted at bango. After a week, I began to have hope that Sergeant Hunt had escaped for good, but my thoughts were too optimistic. He was caught and returned to the Japanese guardhouse.

On the same day as Hunt's return, five American enlisted men were caught bringing food through the fence. Along with three Filipinos (including one woman) who were caught selling food to the Americans, they were tied to a post and left for 24 hours without food or water. The Americans were warned that they should not go near to, speak to, or try to help the punished in any way. One of the enlisted men became crazed with thirst, broke loose, and tried to run to a water tap nearby. He was caught, beaten severely, and retied to the post. They were left there all that chilly, rainy night.

The next morning the Japanese, as if they wished to impress on us now and forever the penalty for trying to escape or trade with the Filipinos, ordered that all hospital personnel and all patients able to walk assemble in the area of the main gate of the hospital to witness some executions. Late that day two Americans, including Sergeant Hunt, were escorted through the gate by twelve Japanese with rifles, two firing squads. Just after the Japanese marched through the hospital gate, the leader of the two squads called a halt and rushed over to the front of the hospital kitchen. There was some heavy twine there which was used to keep open one of the sawali shutters. The Japanese guard hacked at the cord with his bayonet

Opposite: Execution at Cabanatuan.

until it came loose; he then rejoined his squad laughing as if back from a great lark.

They then resumed the march, and one of the prisoners, a red-headed sergeant, turned his head, smiled, and waved at the totally silent audience. The two doomed men were led to the two graves which they had been made to dig for themselves the night before. Their hands were tied behind them with the cord from the kitchen window, and they were then made to kneel facing their graves. The firing squad fired and the men fell, but not into their graves as they were supposed to. The bodies were prodded over the edge and into the grave with bayonets. Witnesses standing nearby were enlisted to fill the graves, already half full of water from the recent rain. Though we in the hospital did not witness it, seven others including the one Filipino woman were executed elsewhere in the camp at the same time. Soon afterward, in early July, the Japanese announced that henceforth for each prisoner who escaped nine would be shot. We were told to draw up lists of ten; if any one person in the group tried to escape, the remaining nine would be shot. No one on my list had any ideas about escaping, knowing what the odds were of surviving beyond the fence, but we did under the circumstances make grim jokes about how we suspected certain members of our "shooting squad" as having a desire to depart. In mid–September the threat of the shooting squads was tested when two men from the same shooting squad escaped from a hospital ward. The other eight men in the squad were locked up, but no one was shot.

Later the same month, a man from New Mexico went through the fence. Fortunately, his nine mates were not killed. Instead he was caught and paraded on both sides of the camp. Led around like a dog with a Japanese soldier prodding him with a bayonet, he bore a large sign on his back proclaiming that he had been foolish enough to try to escape. The Japanese colonel lectured us all this while, maintaining that we were lucky to be Japanese prisoners of war, that no prisoners anywhere were getting the wonderful treatment we were enjoying. He said that his men were depriving themselves of their own food and medicine in order to care for us. We had to listen to all his lies, but at least the young New Mexican was not shot.

We wondered why the Japanese had modified their plan. To be safe, however, the senior American officers decided to see that no one of our comrades tried to escape again, both to protect those remaining behind and because there was almost no hope of surviving outside the fence. In an attempt to reduce the possibility of escape, we established our own interior guard around the camp.

Even so, later that autumn, three officers, Lieutenant Colonel Loyd C. Briggs, Lieutenant Colonel Howard Edward Breitung, and Lieutenant Senior Grade Roydel C. Gilbert, U.S. Navy, tried to go through the fence. Caught in the act of trying to escape, these men were very badly beaten and tied to a post. They were placed by the main gate, and all of the Filipinos who came that way were compelled to take their turn beating the prisoners. I remember the night, a cold rainy one, when those men in abject misery and pain had to remain lashed to a post all night. Colonel Briggs was beaten so badly around the head with a whip that one eye hung down over his cheek. We heard reports that one of the officers was beheaded and the others bayoneted to death. The Japanese we encountered at that time were savage and totally unpredictable.

Because of the absence of medications, proper sanitation, and good diet, we passed a very difficult summer of 1942. In the first part of July, we saw not only a worsening of the dysentery, but a recurrence of malaria in its worse forms, cerebral malaria and black water fever; without quinine the prognosis was hopeless. Sometime in mid–July the Japanese succumbed to the daily pressure and pleas of Chaplain Oliver and Colonel Gillespie, and we were allowed to have church services. In addition they declared that there would be no work details on Sundays. The Japanese apparently figured that church services cost them nothing, and that they could only get so much work from weakened, starved men.

In mid–July we were given a chance to buy some food through a commissary, but most of the men in the hospital area had no money. I had nothing, but the ever-resourceful Jack Comstock had some pesos that he had kept throughout the battle of Bataan and through the early part of our imprisonment. In this first purchase we each got a can of sardines, one can of condensed milk, some cocoa, and some sugar. By early August the commissary had bananas, mangoes, peanuts, and an occasional can of sardines or salmon.

In August the Japanese would occasionally bring in a muddy, fly-covered, freshly killed carabao to supply carabao stew for nearly 3,000 persons. Such a small issue of meat did little to replenish bodies which had such a tremendous six-month deficiency of protein in their

diet. Had there been no overwhelming event of severe dysentery or malaria, this diet was sufficient to allow one to die a slow death of starvation. There was now a rapidly escalating number of patients exhibiting severe nutritional edema and the overt manifestations of multiple vitamin deficiency.

Simply put, the protein in our diet was not sufficient to keep the serum from leaking into the tissues and producing at times a massive dependent edema. The vitamin deficiency diseases could never, in any sense, be attributed to any single part of the vitamin B complex. Instead this problem was a spectrum disease in which, to varying degrees, all of the entities of the vitamin B complex were involved. The most troubling, and most overtly exhibited, was the syndrome of the burning feet. One could identify those who suffered from this problem by their posture and the expression on their faces. The neuritis of dry beri-beri is painful and disabling. The problem was so common that it frequently could be detected by merely looking at the patient. He would be sitting on the ground leaning forward and holding his feet, with an expression of terrible pain on his face. The neuritis affected to a greater degree those parts of the body which were most used – the hands and feet. Frequently foot drop or wrist drop would occur as a result of a nerve palsy in those extremities. Some of the patients would walk with a very uncoordinated gait.

In the so-called wet beri-beri patients it was largely impossible to determine what part of their edema was due to protein deficiency and what part was due to B-1 (thiamin) deficiency. We did see very many in the Cabanatuan prison camp who had edema, shortness of breath, distended neck veins, and peripheral cyanosis. Generally they lived only a short time after the beginning of the abnormal clinical signs. These we labeled as having beri-beri heart.

The summer and fall of 1942 were indeed desperate times for those incarcerated at the Cabanatuan POW camp. Food was so scarce, so poor, and so tasteless that some of the young and less experienced would resort to eating anything in order to quiet their hunger pangs. I remember one event which occurred just below my ward: One afternoon as I came out of the ward I saw two of my charges sitting by a hole in the ground with clubs in their hands. I asked one of them what they were doing. He answered, "There's a big rat down in that hole,

Opposite: The failed escape.

and when he comes out we'll have him in a stew." Any cat or dog foolhardy enough to wander under the fence was fair game; it too became stew. Another time I was passing kitchen #2 when I saw a young prisoner sitting on the ground in filthy shorts, trying to break a carabao soupbone on a rock. When the bone broke in two parts, he began trying to suck out the marrow.

Most of us who survived learned that it was much better to go hungry than to eat food of uncertain origin, but in our small world surrounded by death and dying, we shared an economy not seen back home. When carabao were slaughtered, every ounce of blood was collected in large containers and used, mixed with greens, to make blood soup. Everything about that brew – the smell, the appearance, and the taste – was an affront to my palate. I decided, however, that if I could prevent my gut from rejecting it, I would benefit from it. Intermittently, for weeks, this unsavory item appeared on our menu. (The rice we were getting in late October seemed to be the same old milled rice, but now it was moldy, cracked, and full of bugs and worms. Jack said that he had become tired of picking worms out of his rice, so he decided to ignore their presence. After all, he reasoned, they were a source of much needed protein.)

Our senior officers, Colonel Gillespie and Chaplain Oliver, continued to make request after request for soap, toilet paper, clothing, blankets, and most urgently for medicine, especially quinine. The hospital was visited in early July by a high-ranking Japanese officer, who was supposed to have taken our requests under consideration. Late in July 1942 the camp received a shipment of medical supplies of which the most significant items received were 300,000 tablets of quinine. This marvelous amount of quinine, presumably captured in Java, had to be administered very judiciously. The tablets were only .02 gm., or 200 mg., and there were thousands of malaria patients at Cabanatuan. (Many of the prisoners in the main camp who were not desperately ill preferred to remain where they were and not come to the hospital.) The 300,000 tablets gave minimum treatment for 3,000 patients for ten days, so this token concession by the Japanese was not nearly enough. However, the careful doling out of this meager

Opposite: Dry beri-beri patients were housed in the upper deck; those with wet beri-beri were assigned to the lower deck.

supply did temporarily reduce the death rate, although none could be given for prevention.

During late July and early August 1942 great efforts were made to improve the sanitation of the camp. As expected the marshy areas of the camp provided a good breeding ground for mosquitoes. During this time some of the healthier men provided a workforce to improve the drainage. Indeed, in a great effort to improve our scanty water supply, the prisoners, on their own, dug shallow wells. Major Wilbur Berry, a very bright career medical officer, was appointed sanitation officer for the hospital. His efforts, using his very limited supplies, were successful in eliminating many of the mosquito breeding areas, and through some clever maneuvers he was able to alleviate the fly problem to some degree. But the death toll during those summer months was terrible: 1,500 died, largely because of dysentery, malaria, and diphtheria.

As we endured those terrible months, living in filth, surviving on a starvation diet, and watching hundreds of our friends die, rumors were rife. From the work details to Manila came a supply of rumors, some so preposterous that they were beyond believing. In July we got a rumor that over one-half of the Japanese fleet had been sunk in a naval engagement, and later there was a rumor that FDR had said over the radio that we would be home by September 15. It is hard to know how those rumors started. One sergeant claimed that he was privy to all information by listening to a secret radio passed under the fence by Filipinos. We found out later that the sergeant was lying. I believe indeed that he fancied himself to be a morale officer. In retrospect I am amazed that among all those rumors we never heard about the battle of Midway, in June 1942. Even had the story of the great victory leaked through to us, though, we would have thought it was just another pipe dream buried in that mass of misinformation.

In late July of 1942 we were given a supply of shots for cholera, typhoid, and dysentery. Our headquarters, including Colonel Gillespie, felt that the Japanese issued these for their own protection. (It was hard for any of us to ascribe any humanitarian motives to our captors.) The Japanese were aware that epidemics of these diseases had occurred among their troops in China, and the colonel surmised that the Japanese were afraid of such an epidemic occurring at Cabanatuan. We had no reason to believe that they had any concern for our health. They were afraid that the epidemic would spread to the

Japanese quarters. The day after the injection I was dreadfully sick; my chronic diarrhea became torrential. I was almost back to normal, however, in 48 hours.

During July and August the underground became very active. Many of the men in camp had friends in Manila who would use any device available to get food, medicine, and money into the camp. Very many of those wonderful people risked their lives to help their captive friends. The men on outside work details were the main carriers for outgoing and incoming messages and for incoming food, money, letters, and medicine. The wood and the grass cutting details were most active in these exchanges near the camp, and frequent details in Manila served the same purpose. Some of the most wealthy and influential Filipinos were executed upon discovery that they were guilty of helping the Americans.

The one person I knew who was associated with the underground was Miss Pilar Campos. I had known her in Manila when she dated one of my apartment mates, Ralph Hibbs. Pilar was, along with several other socialites in Manila, a member of the Volunteer Social Aid Committee. She and her colleagues were very active in the underground, and she was very anxious to supply medicine, food, and money to Hibbs, as well as to help others who were in desperate need. The contact of these Filipino women in Manila was a naval officer, Commander Davis, who later died on one of the Japanese hellships. Pilar exchanged messages with Hibbs until she was savagely murdered by the Japanese late in the war.

There were enough rains in August 1942 so that one could stand out under the heavens in the nude and get rid of the accumulated grime. However, many of the patients on the wards were too weak and too sick to enjoy the benefit of the rain. We were able to carry some of them outside but not all. The wards were heavily infested with lice and bedbugs, and there seemed to be no way that we could get rid of them. The bedbugs were an itchy, crawly annoyance that kept us awake at night, and their repugnantly sweetish odor was constantly present. The lice were a natural consequence of our living conditions. There were all varieties of lice present; they inhabited our scalps, our clothes, and our pubic areas. It was not unusual to see patients scanning their clothes and bodies for lice. Those little insects were an added page to our book of misery. Jack was extremely conscious of the infestations, so much so that he had his head shaved. I

have to confess that his hair styling didn't improve his looks. When Jack found a louse anywhere on his clothes or body, his fury was almost ungovernable. He stated that no one in the long line of Comstocks had ever been lice-infested before.

In the midst of starvation and disease, POWs inevitably had a high incidence of tuberculosis. At its peak population, there were 13,000 military personnel in the Cabanatuan prisoner of war camp where I was incarcerated. Many were Mexican-Americans who had a very low resistance to tuberculosis. In 1942 and 1943, at least half of the prisoner population would have had positive tuberculin skin tests indicating either present active disease or past exposure. Many in such a cohort of thousands would, under the influence of disease and starvation, go from latent to active disease. In late 1942 and in early 1943 at Cabanatuan the POW doctors began to report many cases of suspected tuberculosis. Any doctor who made night rounds on his ward heard frequent coughing, not the simple coughing of mild bronchitis but those body-racking sounds described in Thomas Mann's *The Magic Mountain*. The young hero of the novel, Hans Castorp, makes a three-week visit to his cousin, a patient in a TB sanatorium in the Alps. Castorp becomes "suddenly rooted to the spot by a perfectly ghastly sound coming from a little distance off around the bend in the corridor. ... It was coughing obviously ... but coughing like to no one Hans Castorp had ever heard, and compared with which any other had been a magnificent and healthy manifestation of life; a coughing that had no conviction and gave no relief, that did not even come out in paroxysms but was just a feeble welling up of the juices of organic dissolution."

There is only one worse-sounding cough. I had to listen to it as I made my way past another ward to my own. It was a horrible, high-pitched, brassy sound from a young man who was literally coughing up his liver. An amoebic abscess had eroded from his liver, through the diaphragm, and into his lung. The cough was incessant. Unable to eat or sleep, he died in about two weeks from sheer exhaustion.

The problem of tuberculosis at Cabanatuan became so severe, and isolation was so badly needed, that the senior officer decided to create a TB ward. Since I had been ward officer on the tuberculosis service at Sternberg General Hospital in Manila, my senior officer

Opposite: Farm detail at Cabanatuan.

decided that I was the expert. There was certainly no competition for
the job. My new assignment at the Cabanatuan POW hospital was to
visit all 31 wards and, with the use of a stethoscope, ferret out cases
of overt TB. The purpose was purely to isolate, on one ward, what we
designated as "open cases." I had the nagging fear that my limited
auscultatory skills might condemn someone free of the disease to an
open, crowded ward with millions of acid-fast bacilli floating around.
On the other hand, the alternative of leaving open cases on the wards
was worse.

The Japanese had given us an ancient X-ray machine, but our
problem was an extremely limited supply of very poor X-ray film. I
was only allowed to X-ray doubtful cases. The laboratory had an old
monocular microscope, but there were no facilities for doing acid-fast
stains on sputum. My patients were poorly diagnosed and poorly
treated. Floor space for each cot was about two and a half feet wide,
and even when we placed patients so that heads alternated with feet
the arrangement was inadequate: the crowding and the breathing of
air loaded with a bacillary miasma from coughing ensured that those
mistakenly segregated would be infected.

Prisoners with open, active, and cavitary disease had no chance.
Some of those with tuberculosis also had malaria, dysentery, or both,
factors that made recovery almost impossible. Very many, diagnosed
and undiagnosed, died of the disease. Others – including me – survived the war only to discover that they, too, had tuberculosis.

The August rumors were a rehash of the old ones plus several
which showed that someone had a great genius for invention. The
rumors that our troops had landed in Lingayen Gulf (where the Japanese had landed in their invasion of Luzon) and that Clark Field had
been bombed seemed very fanciful. The choicest and the greatest
flight of fancy occurred when it was rumored that the American flag
would fly over Manila in about a week.

One of the officers, Captain Frank Cone, developed a mass in his
lower abdomen. Colonel Jack Schwartz, a very capable surgeon, took
Frank into the hospital of the nearby city of Cabanatuan for surgery,
which was carried out under some very primitive conditions. The
surgeon had to induce spinal anesthesia through a trochar, several
times the bore of a spinal needle. Colonel Schwartz found on opening
Frank's abdomen that he had an inoperable carcinoma of his colon.
Colonel Schwartz left the captain there, but in a short time Captain

Cone was returned to the camp hospital where he died soon thereafter. That was a personal loss to me, for Frank Cone was a North Carolina boy. I had met him at Sternberg two months before the attack on Pearl Harbor. Someone had told him that I too was from North Carolina and he had come to the hospital to meet me. We had a nice chat about home and our plans once we got back there.

In late August all of the generals and colonels were removed from camp and taken to Formosa. Colonel Gillespie, later to be Major General Gillespie, was taken in that group. I surely hated to see him go; he was a good physician and a good officer. He had served very well as commanding officer of General Hospital #2 in Bataan, and had shown great courage contending with the Japanese in an effort to improve our lot in the prison camp. The officers and corpsmen were called to the road in front of the hospital headquarters where Colonel Gillespie bade us farewell.

By the first of September 1942 there were fewer deaths. It seemed that in the three months preceding, the weakest and sickest men had died at a rapid pace. Those remaining, many of whom were just hanging on, were lucky. It seemed that survival depended a lot on where one happened to be at a certain time. The most stricken were the combat troops from Bataan and those who had been at Camp O'Donnell. Of those remaining, barring some severe episodes of sickness, there was a fair chance of survival. There was some improvement in the food. There were some greens in the form of comote tops and talinum, and the occasional carabao stew. Through the fence we were able to obtain some bananas, mangoes, peanuts, and an occasional can of sardines.

However, in spite of the food's being a trifle better, prisoners were beginning to show greater evidence of deficiency disease. Few present-day medical students ever see beri-beri, except in a chronic alcoholic. Rare too is a case of scurvy or pellagra. But Cabanatuan would have been much more than a lifetime's learning experience for one who wished to study nutritional deficiencies and their effects on the human mind and body.

By late September 1942 life at Cabanatuan was at a very low ebb. We had no more quinine to treat the malaria except what was coming in through the barbed wire. Over 1,800 men had died over the past few months. There was even a dearth of rumors, and we were getting baths only when it rained. At this time Jack had begun to reflect on

the history of war; he decided that wars in general were not con-
cluded in six months or a year, but at best were bound to persist for
years. The high point of that month was the few eggs we bought at
the Japanese commissary. We rationed them carefully, calling them
our "little nuggets of protein."

Cabanatuan was a place that perfectly exemplified the old saw
about necessity breeding invention. From the beginning there were
those who very quickly adapted, as much as humanly possible, to their
bleak surroundings. There were the geta clog makers, a specialty in
itself. Others took some of the heartwood of Filipino mahogany and
made beautiful pipes for those who chose to smoke the awful Japanese tobacco. Some of the men had brought needles and thread to Bataan and then to Cabanatuan which were used to mend and repair
tattered clothes. When the thread ran out they would unravel a piece
of material to get more thread. It was amazing how many hundreds
brought a book with them, sacrificing precious space in their musette
bag just to have reading material. If one had a book he had access to
a whole lending library, and he could exchange his book for any one
of several hundred others that were owned by his fellow prisoners.
The privilege of reading a book could cost a few cigarettes, a banana,
a few peanuts, or part of a serving of one's rice. All other services
were traded in the same manner. I read many dirty, tattered books
just for the pleasure of reading. The barter system was very active
at Cabanatuan.

The medicinal agent which we least needed was the one in boun-
teous supply – mineral oil. This may have been a Japanese way of com-
plying with the Geneva Convention. In the face of such scarcity of
everything, though, a use was sure to be found for it. Our diet every
day, every week, every month was rice mixed with a weed-like green
called talinum. In such surroundings, we naturally tried to find some
way of relieving our monotonous diet. I do not know who the genius
was, but someone found a way to make his rice more palatable: he
fried his rice in mineral oil. There was no padlock on the room where
the mineral oil was kept; in an atmosphere where loose bowels were
the rule, who would think of stealing mineral oil?

Very soon the practice became widespread, and the mineral oil inventory, for the first time, began to drop. Had he wished to identify
the culprits filching the mineral oil, the evidence was very visible. No
sleuth was needed. Mineral oil does not become absorbed as it

traverses the gut. Every drop of it pursues its way downward to emerge intact. Since almost everyone had diarrhea, there was almost no impediment to its passage. Very frequently this leak of mineral oil was totally involuntary, and the liquid would terminate its passage by making a large greasy spot on the seat of the pants. The spot was always round, but varied greatly in size depending almost entirely on how much mineral oil had been added to the mix. After this food fad was introduced, its popularity was demonstrated by the great number walking around exhibiting this oily stigma. After a few weeks there was a marked reduction in the number of spots seen around camp. The senior medical officer had spread the word that mineral oil absorbed and removed vitamin B from our food as it went through the gut. Since we were already malnourished, there was great danger in aggravating the situation. The passing popularity of mineral oil pancakes was not at all surprising.

Other variety was provided by a young marine who, by some unknown means, acquired an old fashioned sausage grinder which he used to grind rice for a fee, usually a fraction of the rice he ground. We also at this time were getting an occasional serving of dried fish which we could soak in water and add to a stew. We could see the fish lying on a rack to dry, though, so covered with flies that it looked black. And the smell was awful. Jack's admonition was, "Hold your nose and eat. This is the only protein we have today."

Near the first of October 1942 we were visited by a typhoon. I was used to typhoons and typhoon warnings while living in Manila, but in Manila the buildings were substantial and in no danger of being blown away. Most of the buildings at Cabanatuan were of flimsy nipa construction, and all had nipa roofing. We were in great fear that our living quarters would go, but they did not. We opened the nipa side windows and let the wind pass through. All of the latrines were blown over, and several other buildings blown flat.

The rumor mills kept grinding away. The grist remained the same – grains of truth, grains of fantasy. There was a rumor that very soon thousands of men would be processed for departure to Japan. By now the rumors at times appeared to have some hint of truth, but Jack had been bitten so many times that he was beginning to be skeptical of all rumors. An indication that he was losing faith became evident when he shaved his beard and his mustache which he had groomed with such care. He had said that he would let the beard grow until we were liberated by American troops. When so much of the scuttlebutt, after ten months, had proven to have no foundation, Jack became a non-believer. He said that the beard came off because of lice, but I did not believe him. He was disillusioned. One of these rumors did come true, however: a large detail of men was shipped out to Davao.

In early October the Japanese sent some of their own doctors into the hospital to do some investigation. They were to determine what the medical situation was at Cabanatuan. I was assigned to accompany and assist a Nipponese doctor who knew not one word of English, and of course I knew the same amount of Japanese. As I followed him, he peeked and peered everywhere. He seemed to be interested primarily in the kitchens and the food service, and as he grunted and "Ah-so ga"-ed his way from here to there he scribbled notes in a very little folio which he carried in a pouch attached to his belt. He never smiled, but he carried courtesy to an extreme. He bowed so often — and I was obliged to return the bows — that I began to feel like we were bobbing for apples back in Wilkesboro.

This "exhaustive" research lasted two days, and I am sure the findings must have been all inclusive. As my co-researcher went hither and thither with me in tow, I was never for one moment sure what he was looking for. After a brief visit to some area of the hospital he would pause briefly, take out his notebook, scribble a few lines, grunt the non-committal "Ah-so ga," and we would be off to another spot where the ritual would be repeated. However, for that marvelous bit of investigative work my Japanese associate rewarded me with two cans of sardines, a container of chocolate, and some sugar. Jack and I savored my rewards.

Over many weeks' time Jack carved a chess set from the native Philippine wood, staining half of the pieces with some red dye obtained from the laboratory. Jack labored over this chess set so seriously and so cautiously that one would have thought his world depended upon it. When he finally finished it, he began looking for a partner. He soon gave up on me because I exhibited a total lack of desire and skill. However, he did find a willing partner in Captain Alex Mohnac. They played and argued about the rules for hours, sometimes raising their voices.

In late October we were advised from our own headquarters that everyone except 3,000 patients and several hundred for work details would soon be moved out to Japan or elsewhere. Exact destinations were known only to our captors. We rarely knew where we were being sent until the moment of our arrival.

In late October and very early November 1942 the Japanese were still showing the same obsession with the body count. Another circle of barbed wire was strung about 20 feet inside the old one, and we were informed that anyone coming near that inner fence would be fired upon from the guard tower. One naval officer dropped a container of food when he wandered too near the inner fence. The container rolled under the fence to a spot just within his reach. As he groped for the food, he was fired upon and killed.

The one area of the hospital where the Japanese never held a body count was in the triangle formed by the morgue, the diphtheria ward, and the Zero Ward. They were mortally afraid of catching dysentery or diphtheria, and everybody knew that no one escaped from there except through the morgue. Even the young Japanese doctor who was my collaborator in the big research project very carefully avoided the triangle of death.

At about the same time, late October or early November, the protein and vitamin deficiencies were becoming worse. We were beginning to see manifestations of a deficiency disease which one would only associate with the famine-ravaged areas of the Third World: vitamin A deficiency. This problem of vitamin A deficiency seemed to take several months to develop. It began with night blindness, followed by retinal deterioration, and later the development of corneal opacity. These findings were frequently followed by corneal ulceration and blindness. Many had to have the eye removed after corneal ulceration occurred. Only a prolonged miserable diet could produce such problems. Dr. Warren Wilson, a well trained eye surgeon from California, followed many of these cases of those corneal ulcers. At one time we had over a hundred men who had developed corneal ulcers.

At the same time the other problems such as dysentery, beri-beri, and malaria remained rampant. From time to time, to break the tedium, I still visited Jack on the Zero Ward, although the sights, the sounds, and the horrible stench were not at all inviting. It was still the rainy season and the corpsmen had no chance to get the patients out under the warm sun to hose the accumulated excreta from their bodies. Blankets could not be cleansed, and for days the floor and the

patients made a liquid cesspool. Most of the men on the Zero Ward
had terrible decubitus ulcers on their buttocks, hips, and heels. Their
bodily deterioration was so great that there was only a layer of skin
overlying the bones. Only a few hours of lying on one's hips or buttocks in such condition led to the development of deep unhealing
ulcers.

Jack and I thought at times of volunteering for one of the details
slated to go to Japan, but the bit of volunteering I had done at Fort
Custer was still on my mind. No more volunteering for me. I decided
to let karma make the decision so that I would not have to blame
myself for the outcome, whatever.

While sex was rarely mentioned at Cabanatuan, food was an ever-
present topic. Many of those young men used whatever writing material was available and spent hours on end writing out recipes and
menus they intended to use when they were liberated. Some few actually wrote enough about their food fantasies to fill a large cookbook.
Personally, I never wrote one menu; but I did have dream after dream
about food. Frequently I went to bed very hungry and later dreamed
wonderful dreams about a riot of food. In those reveries I was being
fed dish after dish, exotic and plain. But just when I was getting
started on some delicacy, I would wake up with a void in my mid-
section. Remarkably, I usually went back to sleep and resumed the
dream feast.

Tea and coffee were difficult to come by at Cabanatuan. Most of
us during peacetime at the army and navy posts had paused at mid-
morning and mid-afternoon for a cup of coffee or tea. This ritual had
been a morale builder and was greatly missed. As POWs we had a need
for such moments in which we could chat and sip tea or coffee. A bundle of tea leaves, no matter how poor in quality, was a way to relieve
the tedium of our days. The hot, black, unsweetened brew helped to
drive away some of the penetrating dampness of the rainy season.

My friend Jack and I shared everything during our years together
at Cabanatuan. When we were able to obtain some sugar, a few bananas, or a few quinine pills through the fence we felt lucky. But in
November of 1942, our stock of tea, quinine and other items was down
to zero. Jack had a very expensive watch given to him by his sister
when he finished medical school. How that watch had escaped the
alert eyes of the Japanese I do not know, but Jack was a very
resourceful person. In those bleak days Jack finally decided to trade

his watch through the fence. Jack philosophized, "What do I need with a watch in a place where the time means nothing? If we were locked up at home in prison we would know to a day when we would be released and would attend to the ticking of the clock and the chalking off of the days from the calendar."

The trade was made through an agent. Only a few POWs knew of those "safe windows" in the barbed wire where one could barter with the Filipinos and certain Japanese guards. To try to do such trading on one's own was a very dangerous undertaking. After paying the exchange fee, Jack received 80 pesos for his fine watch. The trade was timely for us; we had been reduced to rice and greens (talinum), dull fare but better than nothing. Our first purchase with the watch money, again through the fence, was a container of green tea.

In the mid-afternoon of the day of purchase we decided to find a place to brew some tea. Jack and I made our way to the kitchen through the sticky mud and rain. We had our canteens and green tea; all we needed was fire. The wood hauled into the camp for cooking was green and wet. Just how the cooks started or maintained the fire was beyond my understanding. When we arrived at the kitchen, the fire in the oven was barely aflicker. We stood, hopefully, for many minutes until the flame under the rice cauldron was hot enough to brew tea. We very carefully added enough leaves to make a cup of tea.

Afterwards we sat down on a bench nearby and without uttering a word savored our treasure sip by sip. I do believe that those canteens full of unsweetened tea, at that time, gave both of us a renewed hope that we would survive. That one cup of tea, for what reason I do not know, stands out as one of the highlights of my imprisonment.

In late October the Japanese produced the needed supplies for doing stool specimens in order to detect the presence of amoebic infection. This one move by the Japanese had us baffled at least for a while. Captain Harold Keschner, a remarkably good clinical pathologist, began the task of doing stool specimens on several thousand patients. We wondered if the Japanese were going to supply enough drugs to control the amoebic dysentery rampant throughout the camp. The widespread epidemic-like disease had more recently compounded our other woes. But our thoughts that the Japanese were perhaps motivated by a feeling of humanity this time were utterly in error. Instead, the Japanese were beginning their move of sending as many able-bodied POWs to Japan as possible. They very much feared amoebic dysentery and did not wish to allow anyone who had it to be sent to their homeland.

One of our big problems was to find enough containers to collect stools from everyone. Throughout the camp hundreds of sardine, salmon, and corned beef cans were used as specimen jars after the wrappers were removed to use for writing paper. There were many who had not the slightest desire to go to Japan, and there was some bartering of amoeba-free stools with those infected with the amoeba parasite. I must confess, to keep the account honest, that Jack and I were tempted to do a little bartering ourselves, but I had decided after my volunteering experience at Fort Custer to leave my fate to a more normal determiner. I truly hoped that none of us ever had a cause to regret having engaged in a stool exchange.

Our headquarters thought that the purpose of the recent Japanese "research" in the hospital was to prove to the world that our health problems at Cabanatuan were due directly to our poor sanitation and starvation in Bataan, thus absolving the Japanese of all guilt for our plight. There was certainly no one who would deny that as a whole we were in poor condition at the end of the battle of Bataan, but no sane person would conclude that Bataan and the Death March had caused all our problems. Any impartial investigative group would be compelled by reason to see that with few exceptions all those lives could have been saved by proper nutrition and proper medications.

Early in October it was announced that we officers would receive our first mail. There was a great feeling of anticipation among us, since none of us had heard from home in over ten months. We gathered in and around the mailroom until someone came with a small packet of letters – a great disappointment to everyone, since we knew there were literally tons of mail waiting at the Japanese headquarters under the pretense that they were being censored. I received one letter from my Chinese tailor in Manila, Mr. Wong, who notified me that I owed him 12 pesos for a shirt he had made for me just before Pearl Harbor. I had been hoping fervently for a letter from my mother, who suffered from severe hypertension and heart disease. One of that scanty sheaf of letters was for Captain Cyrus DeLong, a young dental officer from Florida. He very eagerly opened his letter, started to read it, and promptly fainted. His mother had died. Jack got no mail. Major Bob Lewis had desperately wanted to hear about his wife and new baby, but received nothing. I have always suspected that this mail delivery was another manifestation of Japanese sadism.

It may have been the food, or lack of it, but Jack complained on several occasions that he couldn't concentrate well enough to play chess or do any serious reading. My complaint, and probably for the same reason, was that I was very irritable and my temper had a very short fuse. Major Sitter and Jack both commented that whereas at Sternberg General Hospital I was soft-spoken and very mild mannered, I was now at times hard to get along with.

My former suitemate in Manila, Ralph Hibbs, was still at Bilibid prison in late October. This was a real advantage to him since he was able during this time, through the underground, to keep in touch with his dear friend, Pilar Campos. Pilar was able to get money and some food in to Ralph. I was very pleased when I received five dollars from Ralph through Pilar's underground channels. I promptly spent it for bananas, duck eggs, and a can of sardines.

Around November 1 the Japanese required that all officers and enlisted men sign a paper declaring their true rank at the time of surrender. The scuttlebutt mill declared that this event meant that we were to be paid soon. During the last week in November 1942 we got a token amount of drugs and vitamins from the Japanese, but not enough to be of any real consequence.

At about mid–December our fortune seemed to change for the better. We were able to buy more food in the commissary; Jack and I gorged ourselves on bananas. The Japanese were bringing in more carabao, and quinine was available to treat malaria. We were still having eight or ten deaths per day, however, in spite of the better food. The diet seemed adequate to help the healthy ones maintain their present level, but far from adequate to mend those who were very sick or near death.

In December we were paid, for the first time. We were given the princely sum of $20 from the Japanese occupation printing press, a small concession by the Japanese to the provisions of the Geneva Convention. With the money we were able to make occasional purchases of bananas, duck eggs, mangoes, and peanuts. The enlisted men were paid only $10 of that "funny money." Under such dire circumstances, with all having the same needs, it seemed very unfair to have any difference in pay. A private can get as hungry as a colonel. Later the officers determined that each officer should contribute something from each paycheck to go into a fund to buy food and medicine for the sick enlisted men in the hospital.

The Christmas season 1942 was not as bad as we had expected. December's rumor mill whispered that Tokyo had been bombed. News of the Doolittle raid (April 1942) had trickled through, but we could trust it no more than we could the other wild rumors. We received a shipment of British food and clothes for the prisoners of war: corned beef, canned fruit, raisins, chocolate, and sugar. There was also a shipment of individual food packages. Each one of us received about three/fourths of a parcel, and the bulk food went to the mess hall. The death rate, due to the improved diet and the availability of quinine, dropped sharply. There were now days when we had no deaths. On New Year's Eve we received ten-pound Red Cross food packages that contained very nourishing items such as cheese, corned beef, raisins, and chocolate.

At this time Jack, for some unaccountable reason, became quite enthusiastic about exercise. He and Captain Alex Mohnach put up a chinning bar near the officers' quarters and became quite proud of their exploits on the bar. They also did a lot of pushups and squats. They weren't satisfied to do their exercises on their own, and insisted that I join them. Up to that time none of us had had enough energy to be excited about calisthenics.

On this holiday we had some reason to celebrate. We were better fed, we had more medicine, and there were many fewer deaths. However, when we looked back on the previous 13 months we felt we had little cause for jubilation. In the previous seven months over 2,500 Americans had died of starvation and disease. This number, added to the 1,500 deaths at Camp O'Donnell, was appalling. The Japanese with their deliberate program of neglect and brutality were fully accountable. Our New Year's celebration should have taken into account the great uncertainty connected with being subject to the vagaries of our captors.

CHAPTER 11

Cabanatuan III

1943

The relative bounty of our supplies in December 1942 was short-lived. Our nutritional and medical needs remained critical. By the end of January 1943, for example, following the brief improvement in diet, the dry beri-beri, the most resistant to treatment of all our problems, showed some improvement, although a great number of men showed permanent damage due to prolonged severe vitamin B-1 deficiency. Those with wrist drop and foot drop were very slow in recovering, and in some cases the recovery was not complete. Perhaps the most pitiable were those who were blind or near blind from vitamin A and vitamin B-1 deficiency. The blindness due to vitamin B-1 deficiency was slow in developing, but when it came it was permanent. One of many to sustain permanent damage to his eyesight,

Captain Curtis Burson of the Dental Corps, blinded due to optic neuritis secondary to vitamin B deficiency, would never practice dentistry again.

In early January, too, we ran out of quinine to treat the hundreds of patients who still had active malaria. The mosquitoes still swarmed, and one could stay under the mosquito net only eight hours out of each twenty-four. Due to the lack of quinine and the generally poor health of so many of the men, we continued to have deaths. After several days with no quinine, the Japanese released to us some quinine from a Red Cross shipment which had arrived in Manila.

One of the greatest problems we had in early 1943 was amoebic dysentery. The disease was probably present all the time but was masked by so much dysentery of every kind that there was no possible way to determine the etiology of all cases. Even though our pathologist and his assistants were by then able with added equipment to differentiate the amoebic dysentery from the bacillary dysentery, the incidence of amoebic dysentery had grown greatly. We were isolating cases of amoebic dysentery in great numbers on separate wards but were in desperate need of medication and better sanitation.

The lice and bedbug problem remained as well. Those annoying little pests persisted because we had no really adequate way of bathing our bodies and clothes or of fumigating our living quarters. It seemed as if the bedbugs hid in the woodwork and came out at night to torment us. We tried delousing the wards, but it was only partially effective. At this time the only interest the Japanese showed in our medical or sanitation problems was to make sure that no patient infected with the amoebic dysentery was sent to Japan.

In late February 1943 I was sick again with malaria and experienced the usual chills, headaches, and high fever. Fortunately quinine was available through the fence. Since the camp was never free of mosquitoes, I felt that I had an entirely new case. There were many potential breeding spots for the mosquitoes, and those blood-suckers had free access to our hides at all times when we were not under a mosquito net. I recovered after a week of feeling terrible.

In early 1943 the news pipeline which a year earlier had seemed pure fantasy was bringing us more believable material, due largely to news reports picked up on our shortwave radio or smuggled in from newspapers in Manila by the underground. And interestingly the Japanese, though strictly censoring news of the war in the Pacific, seemed willing for us to know of German troubles in Europe. Thus we knew that the Germans had been turned back from Moscow and stalemated during the winter of 1942-43. We knew also that several German armies had been surrounded and captured at Stalingrad and that Rommel's army had been defeated by the British at El Alamein. We heard that American troops had landed in Sicily. We even heard two months after the fact that the Japanese attempt to invade the Aleutian Islands had ended with their defeat at Attu.

Even so, wildly inaccurate rumors continued to accompany the truthful ones, and we had no sure way to separate them. Thus even good news caused us problems. A period of euphoria would set in, and in our imagination we would have the Philippines surrounded by huge American naval forces, the marines about to land at any moment. When the marines did not appear, despair often followed. I therefore tended to discount all rumors. My friend Jack, on the other hand, still tended to believe them all. He became convinced that the Germans would fold before the end of 1943 and that the Japanese would be defeated very soon thereafter. It seemed necessary for some of the men to believe something.

The medical situation at Cabanatuan held steady through the first months of 1943. By the end of March there were no recent cases of diphtheria and the level of amoebic dysentery was about the same, but we had no drugs to treat it. Malaria still remained a big problem; we had quinine, but the malaria in hundreds of patients had become drug resistant. At times we treated aggressively and for long periods of time, but with no success. We were also having a lot of impetigo and other pustular skin problems which we attributed to our inability to maintain good personal hygiene.

Some aspects of camp life even improved. In early March 1943 we had something added which gave an unbelievable lift to our spirits. A shower was installed next to our bahay to serve all of the men on the hospital staff. There were, in addition, showers added to the open spaces in front of each row of wards. It is impossible for someone who has never been in our situation to imagine how much happiness a few minutes under a cold shower could bring. Since it was shared by scores of men, at times there were long lines. In slack hours when there was no line I would get under the shower with my clothes on, soap down with a bar of Japanese soap and accomplish showering and laundering all at once. It is remarkable how much the installation of a few cold water showers reduced the incidence of skin disease.

The food supply remained uneven. In mid–March Jack and I were doing fairly well with what we could get through the fence and through the commissary. However, the food issued by the Japanese at that time had shown a marked deterioration. There was no consistency in the way we were fed. At times we had some temporary improvement which was soon followed by a sudden drop in the food issue, both in quantity and in quality.

During one of the flush times, Jack, always enterprising, used some of an issue of raisins and sugar to do a little brewing, the first alcoholic beverage we had had since the night of the surrender. He must have had some previous experience in this type of thing, because it was darn good stuff, though Jack and I drank little of it. The fermenting brew produced a beautiful fruity aroma in the bahay which the other 13 members sniffed, appreciated, and anticipated. With so many persons occupying such small space, there was togetherness in all things.

The Japanese even allowed us to have some open air entertainment. Occasionally there was an old movie which had been dug up in Manila, and at other times the entertaining was done by our own talent. When we had movies, the Japanese would see to it that we were also treated to some Japanese propaganda. On one occasion we were favored with a very long movie showing the bombing of Pearl Harbor. The fact that this was, after many months, their main subject for propaganda led us to believe that they had no new triumphs to showcase.

There was a lot of musical talent at Cabanatuan, and under the leadership of one young musician they were able to develop a jazz band. No one was ever sure where all the band instruments came from, but we did know that the band made good music. We were treated frequently to concerts. There were also some standup comics in the camp whose chief topics came from camp life. They were very careful not to lampoon our Japanese hosts. The Japanese really loved the music and the slapstick comedy, and they attended in great numbers.

Reading was perhaps the biggest single recreational activity at Cabanatuan. In the hospital alone there were many hundreds of books passed from person to person and used as barter. Jack and I spent the daylight hours, when we were not on the ward, reading. We read everything we could beg, borrow, or trade for. I didn't smoke, so my issue of those horrible Japanese cigarettes was used for barter. One could get a book to read for one or two cigarettes. Jack and I shared reading material. He was a very avid reader and consumed all print that came near him. I tried to keep up, but was not quite able to. The only book I recall that he failed to finish was *The Education of Henry Adams*. He said that it bored the hell out of him. I didn't think the book was so boring, but I did conclude that Henry Adams was an intellectual snob.

Many of the men had carried in books of their own, but later the books came in from several sources. Hundreds of men were hungry for something to read and made requests through the underground for books to be sent in. Finally the Japanese allowed thousands of books to be brought in. Many of these books had the names of school libraries printed in them, and it was suspected that the libraries were looted by the Japanese to get those books. Finally a camp library was formed, and it was requested that we turn in our books. The books that Jack and I had were in such sad condition that we were not reluctant to give them up.

In May 1943 – one year after the fall of Corregidor – there was still a great deal of sickness in the camp. There were few deaths then, but the same old problems lingered. It seemed that most of the very vulnerable had died but that many more were on the verge of being snuffed out and were only waiting for some new illness to take them away. There were many hundreds who would survive but would carry the scars throughout their lives. The diet was just sufficient in quality to keep many just barely hanging on. We were seeing some new cases of pellagra and some of the cases of beri-beri were getting worse.

In late May and early June the Japanese became more aggressive in their effort to get as many discharged from the hospital as possible. Their demand that 400 to 500 be dismissed meant that we would be compelled to dismiss persons who were far from ready to leave.

In early June 1943 the rains started again, and in a short period of time we were slogging through inches of mud. The humidity was almost palpable, and we suffered greatly from it. We had just about gotten rid of the lice and bedbugs in our bahay when the ants, on account of the wetness, invaded our abode. The problem with the ants was that they, like the lice and bedbugs, seemed to enjoy human companionship. They invaded our beddings en masse. The little invaders didn't bite, but there was always the feeling that something was crawling on one's skin.

At this time, May and June 1943, one could never guess whether the problem was scarcity or Japanese sadism, but our Japanese issue of food was largely talinum and rice. There were rumors, later confirmed, that the Japanese were looting the Philippines of food for their own use and were shipping huge quantities to Japan. There were rumors also that the carabao had been slaughtered in such great numbers that they were becoming scarce. It was confirmed after the war that it was taking years to replace the vanishing carabao. Whatever the cause, our meat ration dropped precipitously. Jack and I fortunately were getting occasional supplements of bananas and eggs through the fence and in the commissary. The Japanese were still paying us, as captains, 20 ersatz dollars per month of which we gave half to the welfare fund to supplement the diet of the hospital patients.

With the decline in diet came a decline in health. We were out of drugs, and all of our medical woes including pellagra and beri-beri were returning with a vengeance. The problem of burning feet was worse, and cases that had been getting better were now much worse. The scene of a cadaverous soldier bending over clutching and rubbing his painful feet was now a common one. Also due to the absence of quinine there was now a resurgence of malaria. We were also beset with widespread and difficult to treat skin infections of an unspecified nature. We had more water to wash our clothes, soap to wash our bodies, and showers to bathe – we even had clotheslines to hang our clothes on. We rationalized that the skin infections were due to a generalized impairment of our immune system sequent to a debilitated state brought on by a woefully inadequate diet.

We had been treated again and again with the exhibition of a very capricious mood in the Japanese, varying enough to keep us totally off guard – occasionally showing a very lax mood and at the next moment reverting to the utmost bestiality and savagery. One poor man in early August tried to escape from the farm detail. He had earlier been a patient in the lock-up mental ward, and had only recently been returned to the main camp. His condition was never very stable, and his intelligence was not great. He should never have been allowed to go out on a work detail. He never got far away from the camp and was found by the Japanese asleep in a hayrick. His body was returned to our morgue sometime during the night bearing the evidence of an unrestrained orgy of brutality. His skull was crushed, one eye was gouged out of its orbit, and his body bore large deeply scored wounds. Both thighs were broken and the bones were protruding through the skin. The Japanese (at least some of them) did not believe in a clean death; an offender was made to suffer to the utmost before he was permitted to die.

Major Steven Sitter was one of the occupants of my bahay, along with 14 others. Steve was a regular army officer, well trained in psychiatry and neurology, whose wife and children had left the Philippine Islands in May 1941. I had had the pleasure of having coffee with Steve and the chief nurse, Miss Nesbit, every morning at Sternberg General Hospital. Steve had always seemed amused at the naïveté shown by this uninitiated young lieutenant from North Carolina, but his jibes were always of the kindest nature. At Cabanatuan Major Sitter still kidded me a lot. After more than a year of captivity Steve, a close observer, noted some changes in me since our imprisonment. "Johnny," he said, "you puzzle me. At Sternberg you were very mild mannered, soft spoken, and reticent; now you're always upbeat; damn it, John, your behavior is not at all appropriate to the mess we are in." Steve was kidding, but neither then nor now could my feelings be explained. I do believe that the greatest mental burdens were borne by people like Steve who had families 10,000 miles away and had no certainty of ever rejoining them. I had no dependents; the only person depending on me was myself. In the summer and fall of 1943 at Cabanatuan, I had survived over one and a half years and had a strong belief that I would continue to endure. Too, I had a strong faith based in my Methodist upbringing.

In July and August there were persistent and seemingly credible rumors that the Russians were making strong advances and were pushing the Germans out of Eastern Europe. There were also rumors of routs of German armies in the Kuban area, where the Nazis lost great numbers of men and enormous numbers of tanks and guns. This all seemed believable since the news of the encirclement and capture of Stalingrad had been with us for some time. We were also getting garbled accounts, both Japanese and American, of the Japanese defeats. The Japanese strangely were reporting the loss of Guadalcanal (August 1942–February 1943), but by their strange reasoning they were making it sound as if it were a Japanese victory. Of course, if one again scanned the maps, Guadalcanal was still a very discouraging distance from the Philippine Islands. I was also amazed at the strange psychology of the Japanese when they admitted on their own radio that the Americans were producing enormous numbers of planes, and conceded that Japan was not turning out nearly that many. Self-styled news experts pored over the maps in the camp library and spent many hours digesting rumors and poring over maps. Jack, who had by now joined the ranks of these experts, reasoned that the Japanese leaders were beginning to conclude that they must prepare the homeland for the loss of the war.

I could not bring myself to trust the rumors, though, especially in mid-autumn 1943. A deluge of wild rumors swept over us: The Italians were fighting the Germans in northern Italy; there had been a devastating earthquake in Japan with tens of thousands killed; the Germans had surrendered; Roosevelt announced that the war would be over by Christmas. The skeptics among us wanted to know *which* Christmas. The eeriest rumor of all was that Japanese Prince Kanoyea asked for American aid to relieve the earthquake disaster. The crystal balls were exploding.

In August and September 1943 we were getting cholera and typhoid shots, though again we strongly believed it was not a humanitarian move on the part of the Japanese to give us those shots. I had become suspect of all Japanese motivations. In late September, after a number of rumors that it was impending, the hospital was moved to the main part of the camp. So many work details had left Cabanatuan camp that there was room in the main camp for the hospital and those who were presumed well, but the hospital and the main camp were separated by a fence. Jack and I were placed on the same ward, and we still had our mixture of chronic beri-beri, pellagra, malaria, and considerable amoebic dysentery to treat.

We got another rumor which revealed that the hospital was to be further reduced. It was indeed reduced to about 400 patients and the number of doctors reduced to 12. I was one of those eliminated from the hospital staff, and was given a very trivial job as pay clerk to deliver to the civilians in the camp their monthly pay. One of those civilians for whom I performed this service was Ted Lewin, former owner and operator of a well-known nightclub in Manila. I delivered his check to him each month; he accepted it and signed for it with no evidence of enthusiasm. Ted had his own clever operators in Manila who took care of him. He was known about the camp as a double-dealing crook and was reported to have bribed enough persons in control to be able to live in relative luxury. He was reported to have evaded many unpleasant details by crossing a palm here and there with money and food. He and his cronies were referred to as Ali Baba and the 40 thieves. He was well fed, well clothed, and well groomed, and had a number of willing "strikers" who for his handouts took care of him. He was the only POW I ever observed smoking a fine Havana cigar. I wondered at the time if Mr. Lewin would, after the war, be able to recoup his fortunes in Manila.

Jack and I were still getting a check each month from the benevolent Nipponese but were able to buy little – bananas, coconuts, and an occasional can of sardines. We would buy the bananas very green and string them out as long as possible. We badly needed more meat. In late October one of the patients from the mental ward escaped by crawling under the fence in broad daylight. Not much later he was found half dead from hunger and exposure. With no fanfare the Japanese shot the poor devil. This was the second mental patient to wander away only to be caught and executed.

The long-heralded Red Cross shipment came about December 1, 1943. We knew that it had arrived because everyone saw it come in, and the men had done the manual labor of carrying it to the warehouse. The Japanese delayed its delivery for several days on the pretext that they were inspecting it. Our hosts also took the liberty of confiscating a considerable portion of it for their own use. There were, in addition to food, much needed toilet articles such as toothbrushes, toothpaste, soap, and some toilet paper, and one item which was totally useless: shoe polish. I hadn't worn shoes for over a year and a half. My getas were served best by putting them under the shower when I bathed. The food, which was issued in cardboard containers, consisted of chocolate, cheese, corned beef, and Spam; there was also sugar and highly prized coffee. Jack and I doled out this food very carefully because we knew that if we in our hunger ate it in a day or two famine would follow. It was rumored, probably in truth, that the Japanese confiscated all of the Lucky Strike cigarettes because they were disturbed by reports of Allied victories printed on the packages. Some of the shipment was wrapped in recent American newspapers which had information about American success in the

Pacific; the Japanese of course removed the newspapers. The Japanese also felt free to go in the warehouse and carry off whatever they wished.

Every afternoon and evening Major Warren Wilson, a very well-trained eye surgeon from California, held an eye clinic. This clinic was attended by hundreds of men who were suffering from eye problems, the most prominent of which was optic nerve atrophy due to vitamin B-1 deficiency. There were also those, but in fewer numbers, who suffered from vitamin A deficiency which caused opacities and perforations of the cornea. Dr. Wilson worked very hard to diagnose eye problems and keep records. Since the hospital area was now much smaller, I no longer had a ward, so I attended Major Wilson's clinic. We saw there a great array of eye pathology, and it would have been a marvelous experience for one who expected to practice in a very depressed area of the Third World where starvation and disease are common. Dr. Wilson realized that he would not likely see cases, such as those at Cabanatuan, in several years of private practice in California. He likened the optic nerve atrophy due to that seen in chronic alcoholics who eat a very poor diet. The most saddening part was that after making a diagnosis and recording his findings, he was faced with having no effective treatment. Quite a number, blind and partially blind, survived the war and imprisonment but were greatly disabled due to the loss of their sight.

At Christmas we received more Red Cross food items, which helped to make our holiday seem better. Jack and I each got a box of raisins, a total of about 10 ounces, and he, the ever-resourceful one, prepared another batch of "brew"; it helped to celebrate Christmas. There were church services on Christmas Eve, and we were treated to a band concert. It was a beautiful moonlit night, and we were all outside our bahay. Jack and I, along with a few friends, were made merrier by the brew. The band played Christmas music, and every note as it wafted through the clear beautiful night air could be heard in every part of the camp, even in the guard towers where the Japanese guards maintained their vigil. Our spirits were lifted, not entirely due to Jack's brew, and I felt that someday I would be free.

The underground and our radio kept a supply of believable and unbelievable rumors afloat. There was supposed to be fighting in northern Italy, and we heard also that General Eisenhower, stationed in London, was chief of Allied forces. We also heard that the Russians were still pushing the Germans out of Eastern Europe. The Japanese were happy to report in the Manila paper that there was a steel strike in the United States, but soon thereafter the radio and underground reported the strike to be settled.

The generally good news, the extra Red Cross food, and the home brew made from raisin and sugar rations helped the camp to celebrate New Year's Day. We began the new year with a census in the camp much lower than the previous new year. Most of the healthy and relatively healthy men were gone, having been moved out on work details or sent to Japan. Our old friends beri-beri, amoebic dysentery, and skin disease were still prevalent. We had anticipated Red Cross medicine for some time but so far had received none.

In early January 1944 the bamboo pipeline kept repeating the word that ten Americans had escaped the Japanese in Davao and made their way back to the States. These officers had reported the horrors of Bataan, the Death March, and the dreadful conditions in the POW camps at O'Donnell and Cabanatuan. These were Lt. Leo Arthur Blelens, Army; Lt. Michael Dobervich, 4th Marines, Shanghai Unit; Capt. William Dyess, Army Air Force; Lt. Sam Grashio, Army; Lt. Jack Hawkins, 4th Marines, Shanghai Unit; Lt./Cdr. Melvin McCoy, Navy; Capt. Austin Shofner, 4th Marines, Shanghai Unit; Major Stephen Mellnik, Army; Sgt. Robert Spielman, Army; and Pfc. Paul H. Marshall, Army.

CHAPTER 12

Bilibid Revisited

February 1944

Early in February one rumor bandied around the camp came abruptly true: The Japanese were going to transport a group of medical personnel to Japan. On January 29, 40 medical doctors, 10 dentists, and 150 enlisted medical corpsmen were notified to gather what we each could carry in a musette bag and to be ready to leave on the morning of February 27, presumably for Japan. Early on the morning of February 22, 1944, we were lined up with our belongings along the fence separating the hospital from the main camp. None of us was eager for the trip because the Japanese mode of ocean travel was hardly the *Queen Mary*. I was additionally reluctant to leave Jack, who remained at Cabanatuan. Our hosts informed Colonel Craig that after our arrival in Japan we would be divided into four groups to set up four hospitals across Japan for the care of prisoners of war.

As we stood there next to the fence waiting, for what we weren't sure, we were given a few cards from home. I received three, all over a year old. One was from Evelyn, my future wife, and two were from my mother and dad. I was elated to learn that all were alive and well. This was the first personal mail I had received for more than two years, although it was common knowledge that enormous stacks of undelivered mail sat in Japanese headquarters. We stood in line for hours waiting for the Japanese to decide when we would move. We were finally loaded, with our bags, onto six trucks and taken to the little town of Cabanatuan. To our surprise we were loaded on coaches – quite different from the cattle cars of June 1942. I sat next to a window. As the train made its way down the alluvial plain, I was able, for at least one-half hour, to look out the window and take a last look at that lovely mountain, Aryat. I had been born and reared in the mountains of western North Carolina, and although Mount Aryat with its volcanic cone and smooth elevation was quite different from the Blue Ridge, it was still a mountain and brought some solace to my chronic homesickness.

We stopped at San Fernando, where at least a few of us were able to buy a banana or two. The town, as we rode through it, presented a sad spectacle. Its dwellings, stores, warehouses, and churches had all been gutted by bombs and artillery fire. Most of the damage had occurred in the early days of the war when the Americans were fighting during the withdrawal into Bataan. When we arrived at Manila we were hustled out of the cars and onto the ground; then the Japanese guards did what they had a lot of practice doing and counted us. We must have been counted for about the sixth time since we had been first assembled that morning preparatory to leaving Camp Cabanatuan. After the bango we were put in formation and marched through the streets of Manila. During peacetime we had been used to Manila's bustling atmosphere with the streets full of calasas, small cabs, and vendors selling mangoes, bananas, and duck eggs. There was always a hustle, a clatter, and the clop-clopping of pony hooves. But now, the streets were almost silent; there were no cars, no cabs, no vendors. Nothing fueled by gasoline moved except for an occasional Japanese army vehicle. Manila was seemingly a city that had lost its spirit.

It was soon apparent where we were headed. That great, grim fortress prison Bilibid loomed in sight. Used as a keep, first by the Spanish and then by the Filipinos, this sinister stronghold had housed and shackled hundreds of political prisoners. Formidable iron gates formed the entrance of that forbidden place. This huge bastion, a relic of former days, was surrounded by a wall 20 feet high and four feet thick. The somber, dirty, gray stone walls had stood through many decades of weathering. Topping the walls were several strands of barbed wire. At intervals around that enclosure were guard towers manned by armed Japanese soldiers. Several one- and two-story stone buildings stood within the compound, all with bare, smooth concrete floors, apparently kept smooth by the many thousands of shuffling feet that had marched there for decades past. The windows were simply openings – there was no glass, no shutters. The central commanding structure was the guardhouse, which we were instructed to salute each time we passed by.

After we had passed through the gates, we were met by a rather officious American officer, apparently in permanent residence. (We were merely transients on the way to Japan.) He wanted us to know the worst on entry: There were no beds or mattresses; we would sleep on the concrete. (I remembered the concrete from my previous visit in May 1942.) He also instructed us to be polite to the Japanese guards. We must bow and salute or receive some unwanted blows. At Cabanatuan the guards had remained outside the compound in the guard towers; in Bilibid they were apt to be anywhere at any time.

The inmates of Bilibid were no better off than we had been at Cabanatuan. These men were thin, pale, and spiritless. Their food consisted of rice, greens, and very little meat. The inmates were allowed to spend a few pesos a month in the commissary, which would buy only a few bananas and peanuts.

One thing not in short supply at Bilibid was rumors, even though the Japanese were becoming sensitive about the rumors and tried hard to suppress our scuttlebutt channels. It was conjectured that the more losses the Japanese experienced, the more touchy they became about news. It was not a good idea to depend upon the "news" from the *Manila Tribune,* which was smuggled in by the men on the work details, because the *Tribune* was under the strict censorship of the Japanese. The outside work details, however, were able at times to have access to news which had been heard on shortwave radios. I'm afraid that some of our troops were tactless enough to flaunt American wins – or reported wins – in the face of the Nipponese. The place teemed with rumors about the pounding of Truk by American planes and our advances in the Carolines. From scanning maps at Cabanatuan, however, I had learned that Truk and the Carolines were still about 2,000 miles from Manila. I could not allow myself to get caught up in this ever-fluctuating flood of hearsay.

At Bilibid we had nothing to do; we experienced tedium drawn out to the utmost. There was no place to lie or sit except on the concrete. We had a watery rice porridge (lugao) for breakfast, along with a cup of unsweetened tea; for lunch we had a thin soup and boiled cracked corn; and for the evening meal we had a mixture of rice and greens soup. Occasionally we had the delicacy of that awful tasting, awful smelling dried fish.

I do remember well the single surprise bounty bestowed on us before we left; we were permitted to get a rather large purchase of peanuts, bananas, and papayas at the commissary. We had mango beans also, but there was no way to cook them, and I was afraid to eat them raw since I still had a recurrent diarrhea. Some of us had tried eating raw mango beans at Cabanatuan and wound up with cramps and diarrhea. I traded the mango beans away to a permanent resident of Bilibid who had a less delicate GI tract. We waited and waited for the word that we were going. The Japanese for some reason seemed to have a great fear that we would know the exact time of our departure, so we were put on notice two or three times only to have the trip abruptly cancelled. They seemed to enjoy keeping us in suspense and off balance.

The run of news before we left Bilibid did not set us at ease. The men in the work details down at the dock area, although not always totally reliable, had heard about a convoy of ships carrying hundreds of POWs that had left Manila several days before our arrival at Bilibid. Two of the five ships in that convoy were reported to have been sunk in the China Sea; the three remaining limped into Manila Bay after encounters with American torpedoes. This picture was far from comforting.

We were finally alerted and with our meager belongings marched back through the gates of Bilibid. As we passed through, the city seemed desolate. At that early hour few people were on the street; and they did not come near us, having been rebuffed so many times when they had tried to be friendly to American prisoners of war. From Escarga Street we were marched down Quezon Boulevard, across Quezon Bridge, which spanned the Pasig River, and then continued through the walled city. We finally came to Pier 7. I had been here three times: February 1941 as a free man, April 1942 on my way to Cabanatuan, and now on my way to Japan. What a difference between my arrival there in February 1941, with welcoming fanfare, and our departure on this dismal morning in March 1944.

CHAPTER 13

Enoura Maru

February 1944–March 1944

The only ship in sight, except for those sunk in Manila Bay, was the *Enoura Maru*. This tub was about the same size as the *Grant*, but whereas the *Grant* had been sleek and well groomed, this boat had not known paint for a long time and her hull was covered with rust. The *Enoura Maru* had no markings to announce that it was carrying prisoners of war; it was clearly a freighter. Before we were loaded, hundreds of Japanese civilians crossed the gangplank to be placed in the forward area of the ship. The *Enoura* was obviously not built to accommodate passengers, and the Japanese civilians were not accommodated much better than we. This exodus of Japanese civilians in large numbers reminded me of the departure from Manila of the *Washington* in May 1941, with its large numbers of American dependents fleeing the shadow of war. As we crossed the gangplank we were hurried and prodded by the Japanese. They always enjoyed prodding us as if we were a bunch of cattle. As we moved along the deck on the way to our accommodations, we passed by toilet facilities that I had never seen before and have not seen since – privies that projected over the side of the boat. One who had to go risked his life, though I don't believe anyone could have sat long in a rough sea. All deposits in those ship-side privies had a sheer drop down the side of the boat into the Pacific.

As we walked across the deck we saw an open hatch with a ladder leading down to a metal floor. At that time I had a glimpse of what was to be the home of 200 men for many days. Our space was a quad-rangle with an open central area; on every side were two-tiered bays about six feet wide and about four feet high. Two of us were assigned to each upper and lower tier of the bay. I was lucky enough to be assigned a lower space with Captain Edwin W. Tucker from New Orleans, who had served as a battalion surgeon with the Philippine scouts.

Our food, boiled rice and unsweetened tea, was lowered by a rope from above and placed near the ladder where it was ladled out to us. Fortunately we had had the issue of peanuts, mango beans, and papayas at Bilibid, which we used sparingly to supplement the rice diet for a few days. Since the papayas and mangoes were perishable, they were soon gone.

After a few days in that close space we developed claustrophobia. We were allowed on deck only once a day, and that was for the main excretory function. Buckets placed on the floor of the central space were for emptying our bladders.

When one felt the need to go above to those precariously perched latrines, he needed to approach the armed guard, salute, and request permission to go out on the deck. With several guards in sight one didn't dare to pause long enough to do much looking, but, after a trip or two above, and from what we could gather from others, we found that we were in a convoy of 12 ships escorted by a cruiser.

My real concern was what would happen if the hull of that ship were broached by a torpedo. Would any of us survive? We were aware that some of the boats going out of Manila to Japan had met such a fate, and there was no possible way 200 men could climb the ladder in less than the time required for our space to be flooded. Although

I did not dwell too long on that unpleasant subject, we later learned what happened when the Japanese transports were under attack.

We had nothing to do except to play cards, read, and sleep; but with all of the noise of talking and the roar of the ships' motors there was little chance to sleep. We had no bathing facilities; most of the water was used for cooking and drinking. In the evenings we discovered that we had some talent aboard, who put on shows for us.

Our being very low in the ship in combination with the rolling and pitching of the *Enoura* caused a lot of seasickness. Some of my shipmates were sick from the time they got on the boat in Manila until they arrived in Japan. Oddly enough, I had been sick all the way from San Francisco to Manila on the *Grant*, but I never suffered one moment of seasickness on the *Enoura Maru*, although I was in much worse circumstances.

Between Manila and Takoa, Formosa, there was one short period during which we had a great cause for alarm. We heard a great clatter and pounding above deck, and the hatch was closed. When that hatch closed, I was seized with an almost panic state. I knew that if we were hit by a torpedo, that hatch would never be reopened. For what seemed an eternity, we were in pitch darkness and heard the sound of many depth charges. After the alarm was over, the lights were turned back on and the hatches were opened. We were sure that we had been under submarine attack, but the Japanese guards claimed that it was only an exercise. Nonetheless, our boat count of the convoy showed one boat missing. We were lucky. We learned later that we had been under attack and that one of the convoy had been sunk. We on the *Enoura Maru* were on the last boat carrying prisoners of war to Japan which was not sunk. (Indeed, about one year later this same *Enoura Maru* was sunk with about 350 prisoners aboard, all of whom were lost and many of whom were my dear friends and colleagues.)

Several times during our voyage I was awakened by rats scurrying across my face and neck. Of course rats carry lice, and lice carry plague. From the number of trips those big rodents made across my body, I estimate that hundreds must have been on board that rusty old freighter.

The situation on board must not have been a great deal better for the Japanese civilians than it was for us. Apparently thousands of Japanese civilians were leaving the Philippines by every means pos-

sible. Several times Major James Bahrenburg, from Canton, Ohio, was called to see sick Japanese children. The Japanese had inquired if there was a pediatrician on board. Jim was the only doctor who was trained in children's diseases. Jim asked that I be allowed to go with him to see the children. We were led to the forward hold where the Japanese were cooped up in little cubicles where they sat or stood on the metal floors with their few belongings (they had no beds either). The guard led us directly to a Japanese woman who was sitting on the bare floor holding a very sick-looking child of 3 or 4. The tot was suffering from diarrhea and vomiting. Dr. Bahrenburg was able to treat the child and instruct the mother in its care. We had been allowed to bring a small supply of medicine, so that Japanese child was treated with American Red Cross medicine. Jim was summoned several times to the aid of the ill Japanese, and he always requested that another doctor accompany him.

After many days of sea travel we docked at the Formosan port of Takoa. Most of what we saw at Takoa was through a porthole or during our hurried trips to the "benjo" (toilet) on deck. We could see that Takoa was a large city with many tall smokestacks. The reason for our stay at Takoa soon became obvious: The Japanese were using dozens of Korean women to load the *Enoura* afterhold with sugar. Since we weren't tied up at the docks, the cargo had to be brought out to the ship in lighters. The loading party consisted of small Korean women who, using hooks, brought the large sacks of sugar on board and carried them down into the hold.

Those several days passed slowly, but we profited by our stop. The gang of small Korean stevedores worked night and day loading sugar into a space right next to our hold. We were separated from that sugar by only a boarded partition that in some way was breached. We filled every container available to us with unrefined sugar. If the Japanese had conducted a search, we would have been in big trouble, but the Japanese on the *Enoura* seemed concerned with other problems. The brown sugar was quite tasty in our tea and on our steamed rice.

After the sugar was loaded, the *Enoura Maru* and the rest of the convoy sailed through the straits of Formosa into the China Sea. We sailed through the Straits of Shimonoseki, between Kyushu and

Opposite: The forward hold of the Enoura Maru, *March 1944.*

Honshu, the major islands of Japan, continuing until we arrived at the great seaport and railroad terminus Moji, on the northern tip of Kyushu. Soon after climbing out of the hold, we were lined up on the dock for what proved to be a superficial inspection. Since previous POWS had been picked clean of all their valuables long before reaching Moji, we were of little interest to them. Fortunately for us they found no sugar. Then came the hurry-up routine; we were taken on a rapid walk to where we boarded some passenger cars. The cars and seats were built for small people, and those with long legs had some considerable difficulty sitting comfortably.

What we could see of the towns and countryside was of great interest. Our train went through a very long tunnel under the Straits of Shimonoseki. The corporal in charge spoke excellent English. He had been educated in an American mission school and was my first introduction to what we felt was a "good" Japanese. He accompanied us through Japan acting as our guide. Apparently the original group was to be broken up into smaller ones and sent to various POW camps in Japan.

Our group of five doctors, one dentist, and fifteen corpsmen were destined to continue north to the Tsugaru Strait, between the islands of Honshu and Hokkaido. We crossed the strait at night in a large ferry bustling with inter-island travelers. From our tatami covered area of the deck we squatted or sat and watched the Japanese come on board. They came singly, in families, and in large groups, all in a hurry, scurrying to their spots on the deck and sitting quietly until we crossed the strait.

When we arrived at the port of Hakodate we were rushed off the ferry and onto some trucks. We noted with great interest that our transportation was fueled with charcoal, our first indication that oil in Japan was in scarce supply. We were driven through the heart of Hakodate, a city which impressed me as something less than a bustling metropolis. Most of the shop windows were empty and unlit, and there were few shoppers. From downtown Hakodate we were carried in trucks up a mountainside over a crooked winding road through and past a large Japanese burial ground.

When we arrived at Japanese Prisoner of War Camp #1, made up of several one-story shedlike buildings, no POWS were in sight. This was the customary Japanese behavior; the Japanese did not wish for us to communicate in any way with the other prisoners. Officers and men were all ushered into a large room where we sat for a while until the camp commander and his aide arrived. The commandant was an elderly Japanese man dressed in an army uniform bearing the insignia of colonel. The colonel presented with a very stiff military carriage and never sat down as he addressed us. He announced that he was Colonel Emoto and told us that Emoto meant "the source of a river." Of course he did not need to tell us that we were also required to stand at attention; from previous experience with the Japanese military we did so automatically. "I am camp commander," he continued, "and if you behave yourself you will be treated well. If you do not you will be punished." He strode from the room, leaving us with his aide, who spoke halting English. Then came another surprise: three corpsmen and I were told that we were to go to still another camp. Sergeant Arthur Mathe, privates Nicholas Vacca and Perry Boyer, and I were hustled out, loaded onto a Japanese army truck, and taken off–to where, we had no idea. The truck wound its way down the mountain and across the city of Hakodate to a little suburb on Hakodate Bay. We arrived at about 4 P.M., March 18, 1944, at Camp Kamiso, which was to be our home for a year.

CHAPTER 14

Camp Kamiso, Japan

March 1944–June 1945

Camp Kamiso was surrendered by a wooden fence about ten feet high. It had no guard towers, and the whole enclosure covered about an acre. As we came into the gates, we saw the camp headquarters to our left and directly on our right the bath and cook house. The barracks, straight in front of us, were about 200 feet long, and divided at the halfway point by a small hallway extending front to back. On our arrival we were greeted by the interpreter, a very stiff and proper fellow who showed us to our quarters. Perry Boyer and Nicholas Vacca were billeted in one of the two wings of the barracks-like buildings, each meant to hold 75 men. Their home for several months was a four by seven foot section of tatami. Forty of those tatami beds and living spaces filled each side of the ten-foot walkway. The tatami sections extended the length of the barracks, side by side, and were two feet above the level of the walkway. Seventy-five men in each wing slept and lived in this 25 by 80 foot space. Each man, his clothes, and all his possessions occupied his space of four feet by seven feet.

After seeing my two corpsmen bedded down, I was shown to what was to be my quarters for over a year. Along with Sergeant Arthur Mathe, I was shown to the euphemistically designated "hospital" – a 12 by 18 foot room bare of furnishings except for one charcoal burner. The floor, just like the bed spaces in the barracks, was covered with tatami. On this floor, covered with blankets, were two British soldiers said to be suffering from pneumonia. Sergeant J. L. Sanderson, a British corpsman, introduced himself. He said that he and the Japanese doctor, Dr. Yaseter, had been caring for the sick. Sergeant Mathe and I were told that we too were to reside in the hospital. All the patients and all the staff were to reside in that one room.

I walked out of my residence just in time to greet the 150 men – British, Irish, and Scottish soldiers – who came in the gate, returning from a work detail. Such voices and accents this raw young provincial doctor from North Carolina had never heard. As they came through the gates, some were raising big clouds of white dust as they beat and brushed their clothes. They had not expected us newcomers, and as they passed some joked about the appearance of that "bleeding Yank officer" who didn't have a speck of cement dust on him. However, they did not tarry to greet me as they rushed to see who could be first in the bath. This was my first introduction to this irrepressible group who somehow successfully ignored their plight. They had spirit, they had pride, and they had a saving wit.

Soon thereafter, when I went to get my bath, I understood why they had been in such a rush to get theirs. The Japanese spa was filled with a chalky looking soup from the 150 bodies heavily laden with many pounds of cement that had arrived there before me. Even though I had been without any kind of bath since I had left the *Enoura Maru*, I decided to defer my bathing for another 24 hours. I left the "spa" and returned to the barracks where the food was being served. There were two courses – tea and rice, mixed with a sprinkling of large red beans. I was pleased: the beans were a welcome addition to one used to rice alone. I ate my ration in a hurry since I had not been fed since early morning, and then only a rice gruel. After my meal, when I tried to settle myself into a corner of the hospital, I found that my living and sleeping space was limited to one square of tatami four feet by six feet. I had to dispose of my blankets, my clothes, and my body on that square of tatami. This was my sleeping and living space for one year. The tatami was much softer than the concrete floor of Bilibid and the steel floor of the hold in the *Enoura Maru*. Bone weary, I slept well that night.

I was awakened at 6:00 the next morning by the clamor of the Japanese guards announcing bango. I had hoped that bango was a thing of the past. But no, we were counted and recounted twice a day, at 6 A.M. and 8 P.M. So accustomed to the count were we that the men learned their numbers in Japanese. The tedious intoning of those numbers twice a day would not have been so much of a cause for torment if the Japanese had gotten the count right the first time, but it was not unusual to have the men recounted as many as three times. After evening bango came a great rush to get undressed and get done what needed to be done before the lights went out. The barracks were lit for only one hour in the morning and two hours in the evening, 7:00 to 9:00 P.M., and bango would sometimes last so long that the men had almost no time to read or play cards before the lights were out. At times I thought that the prolonged bango was a form of harassment. Absolute silence ruled the night until the din of morning bango. The breakfast that morning, my first at Kamiso, consisted of unsweetened tea and rice gruel. After the little time it took the men to gulp down that scanty offering, they were lined up and marched to the cement factory to work for ten hours.

After we became acquainted, Sergeant Sanderson gave me something of the history of the 150 men at Kamiso. At the beginning of the war they had been stationed on the Malay Peninsula, but with the onset of hostilities their war became a very brief one. After a stand on the peninsula, they were compelled to retreat across the straits into Singapore. Following the surrender of the British forces there, the men were placed in Changi Jail. According to Sergeant Sanderson and others with whom I talked, their treatment in crowded, filthy Changi Jail was no picnic. The Japanese, as seemed to be the rule everywhere, were excessively brutal immediately after the surrender. Beatings were the rule, administered upon the least provocation. The food at Changi Jail was rice only, and the sanitation was deplorable. The weaker and less hardy died in great numbers. In the flush of victory in southeast Asia the Japanese did not seem concerned about the plight of the prisoners. The survivors after several months were put aboard a freighter and carried to Japan in the dead of winter. These men were still wearing their tropical uniforms of shorts and short-sleeve shirts when they were moved to Japan. On the terrible trip in the freezing hold of that freighter, many died of exposure. According to Sergeant Sanderson, the food and sanitation were even worse than on the *Enoura Maru*. They arrived on the island of Hokkaido in the dead of winter, wearing tropical uniforms and half starved. The island of Hokkaido is in the same latitude as Siberia; the temperature falls far below freezing for several months of the year. Upon their arrival in Japan they were put to work with crude tools to build an airfield in southeast Hokkaido, at Muroran. They were finally issued winter uniforms taken from the bodies of dead Chinese soldiers in China.

After the airfield at Muroran was finished, the 150 who had survived were moved to Kamiso where they worked in the cement factory. Apparently these 150 were of the material from which survivors are made. They had lived through two winters as prisoners of war, and it was now far from warm this March on the island of Hokkaido, where spring does not come early.

On that first day after arrival at Kamiso I scouted the whole compound. Only one tap supplied the men with water for drinking, washing hands, shaving, and washing mess kits. How those men managed I still do not know. As I walked through the barracks, I was distressed at the scant belongings stowed at the head of each man's space on the tatami. Many of the men had no spare clothes; all they had they wore to the cement factory. Where visible, the mess gear showed great neglect, and I could detect particles of rice stuck to many items of the mess gear. The camp lacked facilities to clean the mess gear adequately. But the visible clothes and equipment were neatly arranged, showing that the men who occupied those spaces had some pride.

I passed on to the kitchen where the cooks were getting ready for the next meal. There was a cauldron for each of three items: rice, soup, and black tea. The soup consisted of water and some kind of greens. The water for the kitchen was filtered in an adjacent shed. The water entering the filters (several tiers of sand) was a rusty red, and when it emerged below it was the color of pale burgundy. I then understood why tea was the drink of choice at Kamiso.

My next point of reconnaissance was the bath, a large wooden vat about ten feet square and about five feet deep. The vat had to be filled laboriously by hand, and the water was heated in an unusual way. There was a simple strip of pipe bent into a U shape. The open ends projected into the bath, one about two feet above the other, and the curved end of this U-shaped pipe was external to the bath. The curve of the pipe wound through a charcoal burner. The idea was simple – the pipe was always full of water and when it was heated there was a constant flow of the bath water into the lower opening and out the other end as it was heated. As I looked at that bath I made one selfish decision: I was going to take a bath before the cement-covered British Army arrived from the factory. I did get my bath, all by myself.

That day there were only six of us in the camp for the noon meal. All of the men from the barracks were given bento boxes at the factory for their noon meal. Their usual fare at noon was about eight ounces of steamed rice topped with either a slice of dikon or dried fish, which they ate down to the last grain.

Contrary to all rules of civilized warfare, the Japanese required privates Vacca and Boyer to work in the cement factory. Medical personnel were supposed to be exempt, as non-combatants, from any forced labor, but it was not strange that they made no objection. Anything seemed better to them than the dreadful tedium of sitting in that camp all day doing nothing. At the factory they had the company of all their companions from the barracks. Boyer and Vacca were rapidly assimilated into that company. Another advantage to working in the cement factory was that from time to time they had to go to docks to load cement on barges. Most of the lads had become such smooth operators that anything left lying around loose was not safe, especially if it resembled food. They had special pockets sewn inside their shirts and pants, and if they happened to pass near anything edible it would disappear as if by magic.

That evening, my second one in camp, after work they again came into the camp laughing and singing, and as they passed me I heard someone of them say in a rich Irish brogue, "I hear that Yankee captain is a proper bloody 'sawbones.'" This pronouncement was followed by a gale of laughter and comments, the latter in about four dialects.

The men had barely enough time to take a dip in the "spa." The entire 150 were in and out of that bath in less than 20 minutes. Only twelve could get in it at once, so they stayed only long enough to rinse the cement from their bodies. After the bath there was a rush into the barracks to line up for their chow. That evening we were served rice and black tea with no beans. We were all greatly disappointed at the absence of the beans. I had returned overnight to the diet of Cabanatuan and the *Enoura Maru*. Sanderson related that the beans had been a nice supplement for many months and that it seemed very strange that their disappearance coincided with the arrival of the Yankees. The kitchen help had been told that evening that there would be no more beans. After rice, tea, and bango, the men occupied themselves, in the time left, with cards, talk, and reading. I retired to the "hospital" where I was to occupy my strip of tatami for many months alongside Sergeant J. L. Sanderson, Sergeant-Major Bancroft, and Sergeant Arthur Mathe. Because of the hustle and bustle and my fatigue, the faces had been just a blur the evening before, and I noticed for the first time tonight that Sergeant-Major Bancroft was black. I very gradually learned that he was a career army man who had served for years in India and had returned to England just a short time before being shipped to duty in the Far East. He had been on the Malay Peninsula when the war started and had been taken prisoner in Singapore, where he had been kept in Changi Jail along with his comrades-in-arms. The sergeant-major was a tall, handsome man who bore himself as a military man is supposed to. He talked a lot about his wife and little daughter, whose pictures he posted on the wall above his sleeping space. His wife was an attractive woman from the Middle East, and the little daughter a pretty mix of two cultures. The sergeant-major was respected by everyone in camp. Before being sent to the Malay Peninsula he had been a riding instructor for British officers at the Sandhurst Military Academy. There he taught the officers how to communicate their commands to the horse with their knees and still sit erect. He also related that his great desire, after the war, was to come to the United States and establish a riding school. I also learned as time went on that he had become a master in the art of thievery. Since he was the ranking enlisted man, he was given no definite job at Kamiso and was free to roam as he pleased. Over the many months that I was with him, I was from time to time a beneficiary of his skill in the art of legerdemain. Bancroft's acquisitions provided occasional relief from the very monotonous fare. It was, in retrospect, a study of some value to me that after the first few days I never thought of Bancroft as being black. We in our small enclosure and the men out in the barracks accepted the sergeant-major without any thought of color in our interdependence.

Sergeant J. L. Sanderson was not regular army, he was unmarried, and when I asked him what he did in civilian life he answered, "I was a clark." I had never heard of that occupation before, but he explained to me that a clark was what I called a clerk. Sanderson had worked for a solicitor, writing legal papers in old English script. He had been called in 1939 to active duty and was sent almost immediately to the Far East. Sanderson was a very bright young Englishman with whom it was a pleasure to associate.

Sergeant Mathe was married, had no children, and had been in the army for several years serving as a corpsman. He was quiet and rather reserved, a person who took several weeks to get to know.

In the hospital we were allowed at any time to turn on the one dim bulb suspended from the ceiling. After bango each evening I held sick call. Not many of the group were ever noted to be malingerers, and only the sick were put on the list to be kept in the barracks for the day. The most usual problems were colds, bronchitis, and diarrhea, but the men did not really want to stay in the compound unless they were really sick. They were used to being with their comrades, and the bento box, however scanty, was better than what the few left inside the fence were served at noon. The sick call was just a sorting-out process; I had nothing with which to treat a patient. Generally speaking, after a few days' rest, the men were willing and anxious to return to work.

Though near Hakodate, Kamiso was not a part of it. Kamiso was actually a little fishing village which hugged a curve in Hakodate Bay. It had no industry except the cement factory and fishing. According to the British soldiers who worked in the cement factory, the native men and women also working there were just ordinary laborers primarily interested in everyday survival and feeding their families. One thing I thought strange was that Japanese women also worked at the factory alongside the men, some of them doing heavy work. The British were not greatly surprised that those women did hard labor since the women in Britain had also joined the ranks of men doing hard labor. Most of the women, like the men, worked stripped to the waist in warm weather.

The Japanese whom we encountered at Kamiso seemed war

weary, with little or no interest in the war. There was little war news, only that the Japanese were winning the war. At Kamiso, I felt as if a total news blackout had been lowered over us like a net. I found that the Filipinos had apparently known more of what was going on in the war than did the Japanese.

The British POWs working at the factory were a mischievous lot and intended to contribute as much as possible to undermining the Japanese war effort. The machinery at the cement factory was woefully antiquated, in constant need of repair, and the lads from the British Empire were wont at opportune moments to aid this ancient machinery in its decline. If the machinery had been of recent vintage the culprits would have had some problem in explaining why their machine was suddenly shut down for hours. As it was, the sabotage went undetected except on a few occasions when they got a little careless and were caught red-handed. Had they been caught in the Philippines trying to frustrate the Japanese war effort, the consequences would have been dire, but at Kamiso they received a cuff or a kick and that was all. There were, of course, warnings that if such "accidents" were to recur, punishment would be much more severe. But there was never at any time any severe punishment.

I have heard individuals who thought they were experts make assertions that the Japanese were essentially one continuous mass of protoplasm all responding as one to the same stimulus. My experience at Kamiso convinced me that the Japanese, though acting more in concert than the Americans, were not an ant army.

Inside, our camp was run by five Japanese. Lieutenant Tendo of the Japanese army had been assigned to Camp Kamiso because of health; a harmless individual, he sat in the office and shuffled papers. Mr. Yogi Katakawa, the interpreter, really ran the camp. An unbending sort of character who had spent many years in America, he spoke perfect English and seemed very intelligent and efficient. While living in the United States, he had worked for Woolworth in New York City, and had spent his vacations at an art colony in the Adirondacks. The surly one-armed Japanese whom we referred to as "Stumpy" had been wounded in the fighting in China and had had his left arm amputated. His mood was always belligerent, and one misstep by a prisoner was enough to set him off. He marched the prisoners to the factory and back each day and took bango morning and evening. Any miscue on the part of one of the "troops" evoked a cuff from Stumpy, though the men became quite skillful in escaping Stumpy's swinging right fist. What puzzled me was that if he missed the first time he never pursued the intended victim. If he were provoked too much, especially at bango, he would make the tired men repeat the count as many times as suited his mood. This was a successful punishment since it ate into the precious few minutes before the lights were turned off. It was apparent that Stumpy, had he been given free rein, would have resorted to more serious physical punishment. As it was he punished us where it hurt, by infringing on our free time.

"Dopey," we called him (I think he could have been better called "Snoopy"), was another Japanese soldier shipped home from China for medical reasons. Reported to have been diagnosed with tuberculosis, he was a dour, morose individual who never smiled. His one most exasperating trait was his tendency to appear and reappear like a wraith. Snoopy would appear from nowhere at one's elbow. Unlike Stumpy he did not go to the cement plant during the day, so the few of us who remained were always plagued by his presence.

There was a young Japanese who was a pleasure to have around. He, too, had been wounded in China and returned to the homeland. He called himself "Yaseter San." He never once threatened physical violence. In his poor English he told us about his wife and new baby.

I never saw a gun, a sword, or any other kind of weapon in the compound at Kamiso. The tenor of those days at Kamiso was such that one believed, without knowing, that the war fortunes of the Japanese were ebbing. The offenses which early in the war would have brought on severe punishment were now treated mildly, though the fence and the miserable food remained. I believe the Japanese must also have been suffering real hardship and real shortages in mid–1944. At Camp Kamiso we were reduced to rice, unsweetened tea, and soup made of greens and water. In late 1944 the Japanese formed parties on Sunday to search the countryside for edible weeds. Occasionally the soups were "enriched" with fragments of our old friend dried fish, and about twice a week we were treated with a piece of boiled dried fish. We needed protein, but it was almost impossible to consume. Frequently we could see maggots stuck to the fish. When I would gag in my effort to force it down, Sergeant-Major Bancroft, who ate everything with great gusto, would instruct me to "Think of it as caviar."

One brief change in our diet came in November of 1944 when the supply officer, "Yamamoto San," brought a large octopus to the kitchen staff. We wondered why, all of a sudden, we were dealt this bounty. We had heard that the Japanese regard the octopus as a real delicacy, so why this sudden munificence? We ate this many tentacled denizen of the seas for several days in stew and otherwise, and none of it was thrown away. Later the young, cheerful Yaseter San related to the cooks that the supply officer had found the octopus on the beach at Hakodate Bay, where it had apparently died of unknown causes. The cooks related, after the fact, that the eight-pronged beast had looked considerably moth-eaten when it had arrived in the kitchen. Apparently we were no worse for having eaten it, but we decided thereafter to beware of Japanese bearing octopi.

At times my sick calls were serious and at other times hilarious. This group of survivors possessed an ingredient probably essential to survival – a sense of humor. The "Yankee Sawbones" was not spared. My accent was one source of their amusement, and they often deliberately chose to misinterpret what I said. The Irishmen made me laugh the most, even during my sick calls when they were wont to make very irreverent remarks about their comrade's illness or his physical makeup. One Irish lad, Private Day, was a real comic. At one sick call, when I inquired of his complaint, he replied, "Doctor, it's me ringpiece." I was nonplussed and had to ask, "What in the hell is a ringpiece?" He looked at me in a way that showed his great pity for my ignorance, and kept repeating, "It's me ringpiece. It's me ringpiece." Finally one of his comrades translated for me: "He means that he has painful hemorrhoids."

Soon after my arrival at Kamiso I realized that our cases of recurrent diarrhea were likely due to the inadequate cleaning and sterilizing of the mess gear. I went to the camp office and explained, as well as I could, to the interpreter and Lieutenant Tendo what the situation was. I told them that if our sanitation were not improved we might suffer an epidemic which could include both prisoners and camp staff. The last part of my appeal met a sympathetic ear. The Japanese were willing to do anything to keep their workforce still going to the cement factory. Sergeant Mathe and Sergeant Sanderson spearheaded the project. With a few discarded bricks, an old fifty-five gallon drum and several wire baskets, they put together a utensil sterilizer that could sterilize all the mess equipment in a short time. Thereafter the men cooperated and we had considerably less diarrhea.

A couple of months after the octopus episode there followed the episode of the pig. The Japanese in a rare display of benevolence bought a piglet for us to raise and ultimately eat. One of our number, Private Oakley, who suffered from a chronic illness and could not leave the compound to work, was assigned to care for and feed the piglet. Oakley was really challenged by his new job, which he gave the most meticulous attention. For the duration of its existence the little beast was given a ration furnished by our Japanese supply officer, and for several weeks that pig ate better than any of the rest of us. Oakley, who issued a daily bulletin on the progress of our pig, remarked that he did not mind the little blighter eating better than we did, since one day we would feast on the pig. The porker grew and as he grew so did our anticipation. For a reason unknown to us, the keeper of the storage room took an unusual interest in the growth and development of our pig. After many weeks that piggy passed the state of shoathood and grew into a sleek, fat, middle-aged hog; our anticipation grew along with the pig. However, soon thereafter our Japanese storekeeper declared that our friend Porky was in such state of ill health that it was dangerous for all of us to be exposed to the hog, much less to eat it. None of us was in a position to argue with our keepers; such moves in the past had resulted in great unpleasantness. So our four-legged friend was killed and buried just back of the camp. The night after the interment a few of the men were awakened by sounds and light beyond the fence. Some, including Oakley, sneaked out of the barracks and peeped through the fence. To their surprise they saw two men digging up our departed pig. A few days later our young friend Yaseter San, in terms as candid as his mixture of Japanese and English would permit, informed Oakley that the deceased had been served up in the village as a delicious pork roast. Oakley grieved – not because of the loss of a pork rib, but because he had become emotionally attached to his former four-legged friend and could not possibly have partaken of his flesh.

As time passed and the Japanese seemed to grow more lax, some of our lads became much bolder in their attempts to slow down their production of cement. The supervisors at the plants had told the men from the POW camp that the cement was being used all over Japan to build airfields. In November of 1944 two of the British lads, involved in a very vital link in the production of cement, were caught red-handed doing enough damage to shut down the operation for the rest of the day. On the following day they were marched to what appeared to be a magistrate's court. The charges were read, the witness testified, and the judge gave them a very stern lecture. He told them that any repetition of an attempt to hamper war production would lead to severe punishment. The two culprits were returned otherwise unpunished and became camp heroes. Of course, all of us realized that such activity two years earlier would have meant execution. Though we received no outside news whatever, it was obvious that the war clock was ticking down, and not in favor of the Japanese.

As the winter of 1944-45 drew near, I became more and more conscious of the physical shortcomings of Camp Kamiso. As the atmosphere went from cool to cold to bitterly cold, we shivered and with reason. The barracks had one small coal stove at each end in which we were allowed to burn coal for only two hours each day. The men chose to have the heat for two hours each evening, from 6:00 to 8:00. The quarters were bitterly cold when we got out of our blankets in the morning, while we ate our rice, and through the day. The only warm spot in camp during the day was the kitchen, although when we had sick men in the hospital we were allowed extra coal. The outer walls consisted of one layer of vertical boards, a little thicker than plywood. The cracks between the boards, which were sometimes as much as a quarter of an inch wide, were sealed by vertical strips of brown adhesive paper, so that in effect we were kept from the outside cold by one layer of thick brown paper. There was little difference in the temperature inside and out.

The snow came early and continued. As layer after layer fell it finally rose above the windows and reached the eaves, about six feet above ground level. It grew so dark inside that we frequently had to scoop out the snow around the windows. The winter brought several other problems besides freezing. The two hours of heat in the evening would rise to the ceiling and melt a thin layer of snow next to the shingles, and the water would drip and drip until the fires were out and the water over and under the shingles became ice. During the hours when the roof was leaking ice water in scores of places, we scrambled to find containers in which to catch the drips. We tried to sleep while ice water was dripping on our blankets and faces. We had no way of solving the problem, but we tried.

Someone figured out that it would help our situation if we removed the deep deposit of snow from the roof. Those of us who did not work at the factory got on the roof with whatever tools we could find and began the task. The frozen snow was so heavy that the roof was in danger of caving in. In order to prove that I was a jolly fellow I shoveled away mightily. All went well until I lost my footing on a slick place and dived headlong into six feet of snow. I was so far into the cold white bank that I could not move. My British comrades dragged me out by the heels as they laughed and shouted like a bunch of idiots. I really did not view it as fun, but I decided to save face I had better laugh. That evening when the British troops returned from the factory, my headfirst downfall provided the topic and the laugh for the day.

I do not know how we endured that winter with its harsh weather and poor food. The steady diet was still rice and unsweetened tea supplemented with an occasional bit of unsavory dried fish or dikon. (Dikon, a vegetable about halfway between a turnip and a radish, grew at times to a length of 18 or more inches; its tops, which resemble turnip tops, were used as greens.) While in Japan, I never saw any vegetables other than dikon, and I saw little of it. I could never understand why we did not get more fish since the fisheries were a big part of Hokkaido's industry and the British POWs who worked on the docks loading cement saw large catches of fresh fish come into the harbor. The only fresh fish we ever saw at the camp were those which were brought into the camp by the scavenging British troops. If Sergeant-Major Bancroft, who bunked in the hospital, was able to get near a cache of fresh fish, some of it disappeared in the blink of an eye. To his credit he never brought fish to the camp without sharing it with the rest of the "hospital inmates."

Red Cross food packages probably saved some of us. A food package if carefully used could supplement one's diet for two to three weeks. This extra food did make our yuletide much more enjoyable that year, and when Christmas came the men were actually given the day off at the factory. No one was able to do any Christmas shopping, but we did a remarkable job of decorating. On Christmas Eve the atmosphere was very festive, with much singing and laughing.

I received one of the major shocks of my life near midnight on Christmas Eve. The four of us who lived in the hospital had stayed up and dined well from our Red Cross food; a brew of hot chocolate was heating on the charcoal burner. When I answered the knock on the door, there stood Lieutenant Tendo, the camp commander, with

Front cover of the program for the Kamiso POWs' production of Cinderella, *Valentine's Day 1945. Opposite: Inside of* Cinderella *program.*

a carafe and four glasses. He said, "Merry Christmas," and poured each of us a generous drink of saki. He then bowed, saluted, and left. As far as we could remember that was the only time Lieutenant Tendo had ever been inside the barracks. We agreed this visit was an omen that the war must be winding down. There were no more blows either in camp or at the factory.

CINDERELLA

present

by

Street - Dixon - Oakley

PRODUCED BY	P. OAKLEY
STAGE SETTINGS BY	H. SOUTHWELL / J. WHITE
MUSIC UNDER DIRECTION OF	V. WHITE
(ARRANGED BY ATKINSON & BIRKETT)	

CAST

CINDERELLA	P. FARNSWORTH
PRINCE CHARMING	E. MARKHAM
BUTTONS	N. STEET
THE BARON	S.P. GLORD
THE UGLY SISTERS	P.E. OAKLEY
	B. HILL
	W. DIXON
COUNT DANDY	M. SOUTHWELL
FAIRY GODMOTHER	H. HARGREAVES
SCHOOL MA'AM	A. LAWRENCE
TRAINER	A. MOORE
HORSE	W. MORRISON
(FRONT / BEAR)	DICKING
MAJOR DOMO	G.S. COOPER
DISC BEARER	HOUGH
	E. LEMMINGL
COACHMAN	
CHILDREN	DYLAN, MORRISON, LONGTON, WEAKLY, OAKLEY, HILL, LAWRENCE, STEET
EASTERN BROS.	FARNSWORTH, PECK, J.C. SANDERSON, W. DIXON

THE K.K. BAND IN ATTENDANCE

DRESSING & MAKE UP - SANDERSON & CRAWLEY

COSTUMES - ANDREWS

Commencing 7.30 pm 14 Feb. In the Coop Hall.

MUSICAL SCHEDULE.

OVERTURE	INTRODUCTION
SING AS WE GO	OPENING CHORUS
WE ARE THE UGLY SISTERS	DUET UGLIES
THE SHEIK OF ARABY	SOLO BUTTONS
THAT OLD BLACK MAGIC	SOLO CINDERELLA
GIVE A LITTLE WHISTLE	SOLO BUTTONS
DARK TOWN STRUTTERS BALL	CHORUS
SISTERS WALTZ	INTERLUDE
SCHOOLDAYS	CHORUS
GOODMORNING TO YOU	CHORUS
ALPHABET SONG	CHORUS
EL RELICARIO	INTERLUDE
LET'S HAVE A TIDDLEY	CHORUS
I LIFT UP MY FINGER	SOLO BUTTONS
WHEN YOU WISH UPON A STAR	SOLO CINDERS
IL BACIO	INTERLUDE
MINUET	DANCE COUNT CURTAIN
LET THE PEOPLE SING	CHORUS
THE SWEETEST SONG IN THE WORLD	DUET (2 princesses)
WHEN I GROW TOO OLD TO DREAM	DUET
HORSEY HORSEY	HORSE DANCE
LAURIES SONG	SOLO TRAINER
YOU MADE ME CARE	SOLO PRINCE
NIGHT AND DAY	INTERLUDE
AFTER THE BALL	INTRODUCTION
SO MANY MEMORIES	SOLO CINDERS
WE ALL GO RIDING ON A RAINBOW	CHORUS
LOVE WILL FIND A WAY	INTERLUDE
MARCH	INTERLUDE
WEDDING MARCH	INTRODUCTION
IF YOU WERE THE ONLY GIRL	DUET PRINCE
GOODNIGHT	FINALE CHORUS
KEEP ON SMILING	CHORUS. SIG TUNE

Christmas 1944 passed and nothing out of the ordinary occurred until February 1945. There was then an unusual stirring in the camp. The British troops were preparing for something, I was not sure what. Finally I was given a formal, handwritten instruction to attend a special Valentine showing of a musical, *Cinderella*. It was to be a dress affair, which meant that we were to wear the best we had. My captain's insignia had completely worn out on my oft-patched uniform. One of the men, Oakley, sewed some epaulets on the shoulders of my Chinese uniform, and another who worked in the machine shop at the cement factory stole time and materials to form the captain's insignia. The night of the performance we were given permission to keep the lights on until 11:00 P.M. When I arrived, the sergeant-major and I were given seats of honor. I was given an attractive, meticulously done program, actually the only one issued. (I treasure that program, and I still have it in my scrapbook.) Cinderella herself was Private Farnsworth, a very handsome young man. Through some magic, and undoubtedly some thievery, Farnsworth had a remarkable costume. His wig and dress would have graced any performance, but his startlingly buxom appearance produced by over-abundant padding in the pectoral area almost started a riot. (The hip area was served equally well.) On "her" appearance the thunderous applause delayed considerably the raising of the imaginary curtain. There were several in the cast, but Farnsworth was the main attraction.

The physical attributes of the ugly sisters and the fairy godmother were little less startling than Cinderella's, but they bulged where well-endowed females should bulge. The horse in that musical had as its front Private Moore, a Scotsman, and Corporal Morrison, a Briton, as its rear. Private Moore was much the taller of the two, and even when the horse was cavorting it seemed to be squatting. The signals from front to rear of that steed were hilariously out of sync. The singing and dancing went on for a full two hours.

Such dialogue and singing. I would never have believed that so much talent was in the camp. At the end of the performance the applause was tremendous. Several of the Japanese in attendance by invitation also applauded. There was encore after encore; the whole play was a tribute to the spirit of my British friends. These men had endured terrible hardships, but the inner man in each one had survived.

That program in my scrapbook is yellow with age and the paper is brittle, but all of the printing is legible. Since it is the only one in existence, I shall keep it well preserved. I could not then, and I cannot now, understand how they found the time and had the energy to put on such a play. The ingenuity and resourcefulness of those in charge of makeup and costumes still astounds me.

A few days after Valentine's we who stayed in camp during the day, including the cooks, were to receive some recreational equipment from the main camp at Hakodate. A volleyball and net arrived courtesy of the Red Cross. We were given a designated hour that we could engage in this sport. Sergeants Sanderson and Mathe and privates Oakley and Farnsworth soon had the posts up and the net hung. Our volleyball court was between the Japanese office and the barracks. The net was strung from a post just in front of the entrance to the Japanese office and the entrance to the barracks. Our play was very energetic, if far from skillful. The atmosphere was still chilly, and the Japanese kept a coal fire in their office. The pipes to that stove rose about six feet above the roof and were loosely suspended by guywires. As we played I noted that Bancroft kept eyeing that stovepipe and I finally divined what that puckish sergeant-major had in mind: a replay of the scene I had witnessed at Fort Knox. Before I could utter a word he put his thoughts into action: Bancroft was up to serve and he put all force possible behind that serve. The ball struck the pipe solidly and left it in at least four sections, none of which was connected to the stove. There must have been a lot of soot accumulated in that pipe, and at least half of it blackened the atmosphere inside the office. Those Japanese came out of that office, their faces blackened with soot, sputtering, coughing, and swearing in their native tongue. Sergeant Bancroft and our entire outfit were solidly berated, but that was the last we heard of it, and our volleyball privileges were not rescinded.

Hokkaido is much different in climate from the lower islands of Kyushu and Honshu, where farmers can harvest two rice crops each year and grow oranges. Hokkaido has a very long winter season during which the island is under a deep layer of snow for months at a time, and only one crop in the short warm season is possible. It seemed to us at Kamiso that the snow would never go and that we would never be warm again.

In April we were excited by the drone of what seemed to be hundreds of planes going over. They were flying so high that no one could identify them. A few minutes afterwards when we no longer heard the planes, we heard loud booming noises for many minutes. Everyone in our camp believed that someplace was getting the hell bombed out of it.

In the early months of 1945 the front gates were no longer closed during the day, and anyone near the gate could see the Kamiso villagers passing by. On one occasion, in late April, I was standing near the gates when there came the steady drone of many planes passing over. As the din of the planes continued, the Japanese passing by pointed up toward the clouds and very excitedly began to shout, "Bi nigi ku," Japanese for B-29. The last model of American bomber I had known was the B-17, so I surmised "Bi nigi ku" to be an American plane of late model. This was great news, but we were afraid that a constant bombing of Japan and the invasion of Japan by Americans would not bode well for the prisoners.

In June of 1945, Camp Kamiso belatedly received a chest of medicine which contained a supply of what we could only have dreamed of at Cabanatuan. There were vitamins singly, in combination, and for hypodermic and intravenous use. On every sick call I handed out vitamins. There was no doubt that all of the men at Camp Kamiso could use them, although no great number of the men showed visible evidence of deficiency. They had been through a rough winter during which their diet was miserable, so I decided to give an intense course of vitamins. They responded well, but some of them developed enormous appetites which they could not satisfy.

Soon after we got the chest of medicine we were informed on one day that we would leave the next morning for a dock area in the upper Hakodate Bay. We were to take nothing but our personal belongings. The Red Cross medicine was to be left behind, but we were promised that there would be plenty where we were going. Since the Japanese had no inventory of the Red Cross medicine, Sergeant Sanderson, Sergeant Mathe, and I decided to conceal as much medicine as possible inside a couple of pillows and two or three cushions. Sanderson and Mathe energetically set about stuffing the pillows and cushions and had barely finished the job when in walked Dopey, the Japanese shadow. He nosed around for a while and finally felt one of the cushions, which was suspiciously lumpy. He tore open the cushion, exposed the medicine, and immediately started a harangue in his native tongue. He then hustled out of the hospital straight for the Japanese headquarters. We were expecting an almost immediate visit from the camp commander, but he never came.

The next morning very early we were marched to the docks and loaded onto a large barge, riding for about three hours until we reached another dock on the bay. We were unloaded and taken to a large bleak warehouse, a wide open, empty shell of a building. The floor was covered with litter, and there was a strong fetid odor. Young Yaseter San, the ever-informative, told us that the building had been used until recently to house Chinese prisoners of war who had apparently not been able to maintain good sanitation. We were served our rice and tea at about 8 P.M., and afterwards while I was holding sick call using the purloined medicine I was summoned by Colonel Emoto, the overall head of Camp Hakodate and Camp Kamiso. I was expecting to get a harsh reprimand for having tried to steal our own Red Cross medicine. He really talked down to me, but he did not mention medicine. I was told later by the interpreter, Yoji, that the colonel had not taken kindly to my approaching him with my hands in my pockets. Yoji informed me that addressing a Japanese gentleman with hands in pocket was considered an insult; having never read the Japanese version of Emily Post, I was only trying to keep my hands warm. Colonel Emoto's message was that we were not going to remain where we were, but were going back to Kamiso. I bowed to the colonel and returned to sick call. We were all elated because Kamiso was a resort hotel compared to this place. We slept in that vermin infested spot until the next morning. After our rice gruel, we boarded the barge and returned to Kamiso where we were to find things just as we left them.

CHAPTER 15

Camp Bibai, Japan

July 1945–August 1945

In early July 1945, half of the men in Camp Kamiso were suddenly informed that they were to depart the following morning for parts unknown to anyone except the Japanese. (This great penchant for secrecy about very trivial things always amazed me.) Later were found that they were bound for Bibai to work in the coal mines. The Japanese apparently used no rule to determine who would leave, and many close friends were separated. A very short time thereafter, the remainder of the men at Camp Kamiso were given an overnight alert to be ready to leave in the morning, the exact time and destination unknown. The next morning we were lined up in formation; as we started to march out of the gate, Lieutenant Tendo walked to within three or four paces of me and saluted. I was dumbfounded for a

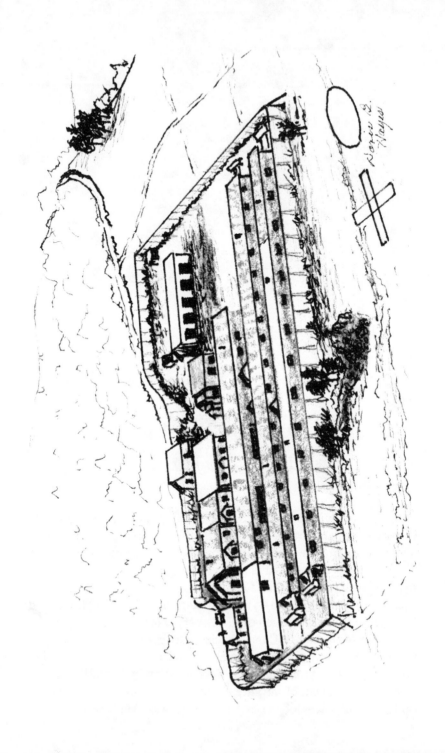

moment, and then recovered my presence of mind enough to return the salute. As we marched out of the gate one of the lads from Blighty (England) remarked, "What the bloody hell? This bleedin' war must be over." Three years earlier at Cabanatuan they were prodding me in the rear with a bayonet, and now they were saluting me.

We were taken by trucks, charcoal powered, to the train in Hakodate, where we waited an hour or more. Some of us had to visit the loo. I was using that facility, along with several others, when I heard the swish of mops behind me. I looked over my shoulder to see two young Japanese females just behind us mopping the floor, totally oblivious to our presence. Customs here were certainly much different from those in Millers Creek, North Carolina.

We arrived at Bibai late that evening, a camp much the same as Kamiso except far larger. There were 450 prisoners, including Americans, Dutch, British, and a very lively group of Australians.

There were no guard towers at Bibai. The camp was surrounded by a ten-foot fence and had only two interior guards who carried rifles. The men were to work in a coal mine ten hours a day. We found soon that as poor as the food had been at Kamiso, it was much worse at Bibai. Our diet consisted of rice, greens, tea, and a rare sliver of dried fish. The greens were talinum, camote tops, and presumably edible wild weeds. In a short time it became obvious that on this awful diet and ten hours per day in the coal mine we would not endure long. Fortunately we had been allowed to bring our medicine chest along with us and were able to dole out some vitamins, but these were no substitute for protein.

We held sick call for one and a half to two hours after our evening rice; the dispensary was flooded with sick, exhausted, and disheartened men. Some of the same old problems we had seen in the Philippines began to appear: dysentery, malaria, protein deficiency, and various vitamin deficiencies. We contended with many new cases of swollen feet. I supposed that since the edema migrated to their faces and buttocks while they were lying down, the swelling was due to an absence of protein in our diet. Fortunately we did have the vitamins and some drugs to treat dysentery, but no amount of vitamins and dysentery medicine could have repaired the physical depletion brought on by backbreaking labor in the mines and absence of protein.

Opposite: The POW camp at Bibai.

Captain Bristow of the Australian army and I were the doctors at
Bibai, and we kept as many men in camp as we dared so that they
might rest their tired bodies. Captain Harry Brown, U.S. Army Dental Corps, did a real service in caring for the dental needs, which were
many, with the most archaic of equipment. Dr. Brown worked with
a corpsman who kept the treadle moving and the drill turning.

One evening in early August we were served some clams in the
shell. Those clams must have come a long way without ice or refrigeration; when I picked my own private clam up and started to open
it, the stench so offended my sense of smell that I almost vomited.
Many others were similarly affected, but some of the hardier and
hungier lads ate the repulsive morsel and became very ill, though
none fatally.

Up to the middle of August we were getting so low on medications that we had to use them very sparingly and only for those in the
greatest need. A great number of the men began to complain about
loss of vision. The most logical conclusion was that they had an optic
nerve deterioration due to lack of vitamin B-1. The lighting in the barracks was very poor, but most of the men who wanted to read or play
cards had earlier been able to do so. Now, however, many were com-
plaining that they could no longer read or see to play cards.

The working conditions at the mines were lamentable. The prisoners had to ride as far as two miles beneath the earth to reach the
face, and the roof was so low as they rode that no one could stand up.
The shoring up of the roof was so poorly done that cave-ins were frequent. When the men did reach the face they were able to stand up,
but they were forced to work while standing in water. The sanitation
was equally miserable; there were no toilet facilities, so the men
simply had to go to a designated spot to relieve themselves. The foul
air due to poor ventilation and the stench due to the lack of sanitation
had many very sick at the end of the day. In spite of all the starvation,
exhausting labor, and miserable food, their spirits were never broken. As they marched into the camp, we could hear them singing.
Amazingly, we had no deaths; these men were destined to survive.

In mid–August three British prisoners got over the poorly
guarded fence and escaped. Escape is a poor word for what they did.
I could never have imagined just where one would go if he went over
the fence. We were in very mountainous country at Bibai, and an
English-speaking Caucasian would have stood out like red drawers on

a country clothesline. Surprisingly, those men were out for three days until the Japanese guards marched them in and triumphantly exhibited them for everyone. We were all drawn up in formation to witness this event. Not a finger was laid on those men, but we were all given a lecture on the futility of trying to escape. No punitive action of any kind was taken. This occurrence, and the almost daily drone and throb of large bombers passing, followed by the sound of explosions many miles away, led us to deduct that we were nearing the end of the war. We did not see the bombers, and we did not know for sure that they were American, but we were quite confident that the Japanese weren't bombing themselves.

In early August the Japanese made an effort to camouflage the camp by doing some painting on the roofs. The painting was never finished, and when aerial photos were taken after the surrender by the U.S. Air Force the "camouflage" made the camp stand out very clearly. In another sign that something was happening, the Japanese kept back large numbers of men from work in the mines to dig air raid trenches.

There was one very surly Japanese guard at Bibai who had not gotten the word that Japan was losing the war. The prisoners had nicknamed him "Groucho." This young Japanese soldier wandered the barracks as Dopey had done at Kamiso. He was wont on the least provocation to cuff one behind the ear or any other spot within his reach. The men learned quickly to signal in some way the presence of Groucho in the barracks. He knew a little English, and was forever trying to tell the men just how stupid he thought they were. The prisoners, as a result of the poor diet and overwork, were getting quite testy, and I was afraid that someone provoked beyond bearing might swing back, but these men were conditioned over more than a three-year period to know what might happen if they struck back or in any way defied the Japanese military. They had seen men beheaded for the least attempt at reprisal.

CHAPTER 16

Freedom

August 1945

On August 18, 1945, I was sitting in the dispensary trying to make some permanent records for the POWs at Bibai, when there was a knock on the door. "Come in," I said. In walked two Japanese officers, which I thought most unusual since the Japanese did not customarily knock. Their message, in halting English, was that the war was over.

I was so overwhelmed that I dropped my head, beat the table with my fist, and cried unashamedly. I didn't need to ask who had won. The signs since early 1944 had unmistakably indicated that the Japanese fortunes were ebbing. Our hosts did not tell us just what had happened to bring about the conclusion of the conflict, but late that day the Japanese colonel who was in charge of several camps, Colonel Emoto, arrived in his charcoal powered car and ordered an assembly in ranks. When we were lined up and waiting, he launched into a long tirade about the terrible unmilitary tactics employed by the Americans to bring the war to a close. Not a word was said about an atomic bomb. He never stated that the Allies had won, but he finally did say that very soon we would be contacted by a representative from our armed forces. Then he added that we were free. Needless to say, the prisoners were exultant. Prior to this announcement, I had hunkered down to wait it out. I knew from history that even when wars seemed to be ending, they could drag on for months or years. I believed that should Japan be invaded and the war continued for a year, very few of us would survive. It is something of a contradiction, perhaps, but I believe that the atomic bomb saved my life and the lives of thousands more Allied prisoners.

Now that the shoe had changed feet, we felt that we were in a position to make demands. Captain Bristow and I marched into the Japanese headquarters and demanded that they scour the countryside and bring in some decent food. They looked at us blankly and promised to fill our request.

The evening of the first day of our freedom, freedom from the Japanese and freedom from the coal mines, the men celebrated in a quiet way. After sundown we had had a visit in the barracks from Groucho, who went about the barracks looking for the men he had hit. He went up to some of the men and begged them to hit him or otherwise retaliate, but no one struck Groucho a single blow. Every one of them laughed and turned their backs on him. I was proud of them; they could not have administered a more severe punishment.

The Japanese were advised, soon after the surrender, that they must reveal the location of all the prisoners of war camps and secure their safety until the men could be removed or repatriated. On the third day after the announcement of the Japanese surrender, American planes flew over and dropped a note alerting us to watch out for a drop of food and supplies, adding that we were to stay clear of the drop zone for our safety. In a large open area below the camp we placed sheets in the form of a cross which was to serve as a target for parachutes. Soon thereafter the sky was full of parachutes carrying large bundles that landed very near to the cross we had put down. Several, however, went astray and landed in the compound. One of the lads, too ill to come outside and enjoy the aerial show, was quite shocked when a huge bundle of canned food came through the ceiling and

Food drop at Bibai POW camp.

landed just beside him on the tatami. He said later that he had been praying three years for good food, but he had never expected the Lord to deliver it in such a manner.

I was standing just above the camp, but inside the fence, watching this delivery. The parachutes as they came down seemed to float as gently as feathers. One of the British lads had the same illusion. He saw one of the bundles coming down in such a smooth, easy, and seemingly gentle descent that he ran forward and seemed, in a playful way, to be trying to embrace the bundle. The several hundred pounds of canned goods hit his right thigh with such force that he was pinned to the ground in agony. He was fortunate: had the bundle struck his chest he would have been killed at once. I commandeered a truck to take him to Bibai, where there was a doctor's office and an X-ray machine. We carried the injured man into the doctor's office and were met by a very elderly Japanese doctor who gave us a long series of bows and ushered us into his office. The good doctor knew a little English, so I was able with words and gestures to tell him what had happened and where the trouble lay. In the office was what must have been the earliest in the lineage of X-ray machines. For some reason that I could not understand he poured what seemed to be a half gallon of oil into a cylinder in the machine and rushed around trying to get the patient into position to shoot the picture; but just as he got ready to snap the picture all of his oil had drained out into a container below. He kept repeating the process until he was able to get ahead of the leak and take a picture. One of my friends, a radiologist, told me nearly 50 years after the fact that the oil was used to dissipate heat and keep the stationary anode from burning out. He explained that the old machine must have had a major leak which the Japanese doctor had trouble keeping ahead of. The successful X-ray shots showed a clean break and we were able to put on an ugly, bulky cast.

We tried very hard, Dr. Bristow and I, to instruct the free captives to enter this new world of plenty gradually, but practically no one listened. After all those months of starvation they were in no mood to fast. Some, in their over-indulgence, did get sick, but none seriously. We were quite well fed, and not very many were attending my sick call.

Several of the men from the camp at Nisi-Asibetu who had also been at Kamiso came to Bibai in a truck they had taken over. I was quite overcome when they presented me with a tribute (see Appendix) which I would have liked very much to deserve. I believe they were so exhilarated over their release that they became over-generous. The little document was signed by everyone who had been at Kamiso. I think that I must have been suffering from some emotional instability because for the second time in four days I shed tears. On that same day the overflying bombers parachuted a walkie-talkie into the camp and some few were privileged to transmit. I said only a few words to identify myself and send greetings to the folks back home. The transmission was a little garbled and my hometown was transmitted as Hillsborough, North Carolina, instead of Wilkesboro.

On the fifth day a group of us were carried out of Bibai by a Japanese army truck to a railway station and transported by train to Atsugi airfield. On the train to Atsugi we were allowed to sit anywhere on the train that we wished. I took a seat in the rear car where there were several Japanese civilians. On that trip I witnessed something I had not seen since I was a child attending church in Wilkes County. There was a rather attractive Japanese woman who got on the train at the same time as did my group. She had in her lap a handsome little baby of about six months who looked around with his very dark unblinking eyes at the passing scene. The woman very casually and with no sign of embarrassment exposed a well rounded breast, and the little tyke rose to his meal like a mudcat rising to bait. All of this scene occupied only a moment or two, and I averted my gaze quickly to view the scenery. The episode reminded me of my childhood days in North Carolina when the church services were long and a baby's hunger took precedence over modesty.

At Atsugi, I was billeted with several of the men from the camp at Bibai in what had been barracks for a wing of the Japanese Air Force. The windows in my room overlooked a large concrete landing field. We had been instructed to remain in our quarters except at mealtime, so I only saw my friends from Kamiso and Bibai for a few minutes three times a day. They had segregated the British from the American prisoners of war, for what reason I could not ascertain. The food in that Japanese barracks was good, but I was lonely; I would have liked to be quartered with my friends from Blighty. The first morning I was awakened by the sound of marching feet and loud voices shouting orders. When I looked out of the window, I saw about 500 Japanese airmen goose-stepping in formation while an officer shouted commands. I had thought the only goose-stepping was done in Germany, but apparently I was mistaken.

On the second night a couple of Air Corps lieutenants knocked on my door and asked me to join them in a poker game, but when I told them I hadn't seen a paycheck for 46 months they dropped the subject. They did tell me to look out the window at a plane which was parked on the landing field. They said that it was their plane, a converted B-26, in which they were to carry me and several other American POWs to Okinawa. Those energetic, enthusiastic young lieutenants were billeted next door to me and I could tell they were in a celebratory mood. It had been a long war for them, too, and they were in a mood to relax. I asked them when we would be leaving, but they informed me that they had not as yet received orders. For three nights they played poker and drank saki while the plane sat on the field. My "flyboy" friends played at night and slept all day, and to increase my anxiety they never went near the plane. My disquiet reached its height when one of them very casually related that one of the planes carrying Dutch prisoners of war had accidentally opened the bomb bay and dropped 26 of them into the Pacific. I thought at that moment, "Here I have survived for nearly four years; what an ending it would be if I had to go swimming in the Pacific." On the fourth day we were loaded onto that plane and became airborne, bound for Okinawa. In spite of their three nights of celebration our young pilots were clear-eyed and eager. During the flight the navigator called me up front to see a vast array of navy ships below, hundreds of ships in formation: destroyers, cruisers, battleships, and flattops, spread out over a vast amount of ocean. I could never have conceived of such a vast array of ships, and I wondered if many navy personnel, except for the Naval Air force, had ever seen the navy from such vantage.

After a few hours we landed on Okinawa and were carried by van to the RAMP (recovered army military personnel) encampment. We were lodged in tents on a soggy hillside turned into a bog by heavy rainfall. Every step we took we sank into the hillside and picked up mud. We had to march through about 400 yards of this morass to get to the mess line. We ate only one meal there and in a short time were again airborne for Manila. As we approached Manila I was asked to come up front to see what had happened to that city during the Japanese occupation and the American bombardment of the city. The pilot flew low, circling the city, and I was appalled at the ruin. The walled city had almost been bombed out of existence; Sternberg General Hospital was flattened and burned; Manila Bay was full of the ghosts of dead ships; topside Corregidor was leveled. I could see nothing familiar.

Upon arrival we were carried by bus to another tent city where several hundred repatriates were being processed. This sorting out of men took several days. We were given new uniforms and documented preparatory to being transported to the States. I visited with many of my old friends from Sternberg, Bataan, and Cabanatuan; I also wrote a few letters. I did not care to visit in Manila, because the Manila I knew was gone.

I was witness to a scene which perhaps tells something about the paradoxes inherent in human nature. There were several Japanese prisoners assigned to our tent city to maintain sanitation in the area. Among the recovered Allied personnel was one soldier, a corporal, who had been pointed out to me as a notorious informer at Camp Hakodate. This man had caused many British and American prisoners to be severely beaten by the Japanese guards and was perhaps responsible for a death or two. For being a rat he had received special treatment from the Japanese in the way of food and freedom from harassment. This corporal saw a few Japanese prisoners passing by on a camp detail, and for no apparent reason jumped on one of the Japanese and began to beat him. The Allied soldier was restrained and led away by several of the American ex-prisoners. The commander of the repatriation related that there was no other instance of Americans trying to abuse the Japanese prisoners.

After five days at the RAMP settlement in Manila, we were loaded on the U.S.A.T. *Yarmouth* and set sail for San Francisco. We made one stop at Kwajalein. It was there, while we were anchored offshore, that I posted a letter to Evelyn, the girl I was greatly interested in before the war. Nearly five years was a long time in the life of a romance, so my letter was tentative and probing. After all, she might have found someone of more interest to her than I. I indicated that I wanted to resume our friendship. While in camp I had heard and known of many who had received "Dear John" letters, so I was wary.

CHAPTER 17

Different Paths

In Manila I had tried very hard to find out what had happened to some of my friends. We had been split up and sent into so many different directions that it would require months or years to ferret out all of that information. For all of us in the Philippines the road had forked many times and the road taken was not of choice but of fate. At the end of that road, the outcome seemed to reveal the capriciousness of fate. Some of the bravest and most promising had been channeled down the forks of that road to a terrible conclusion.

My friend since before the war, Lieutenant Jay Ryan, never made it home. He had so much enthusiasm for life. He served well and with distinction in Bataan, he endured the Death March, he suffered the starvation and diseases at Cabanatuan, and it would have seemed he had experienced all the wretchedness that life could deal. However, in December of 1944 he was one of many hundred Americans selected to be moved from Cabanatuan in the Philippines to Japan. He was first on the *Oryoku Maru*. The *Oryoku*, which was not marked as a ship carrying human cargo, was sunk by American bombers, but Jay was able to swim ashore at Olongapo Naval Yard – miraculous because he had been ravaged and weakened by malaria and dysentery. He and many others were held there on a tennis court until December 23, 1944. They were then taken by the Japanese to San Fernando La Union and were placed on the *Brazil Maru*, which afterwards was named as one of the hellships. The men were forced into a hold where they lived under indescribable conditions. Hundreds on that ship died of wounds, starvation, and disease. Jay Ryan, the man who wanted to be a professional soldier, died of starvation and dysentery while the ship was approaching Moji, Japan. His body was thrown overboard.

Cyrus D. Long from Live Oaks, Florida, had occupied the same stateroom with me on the U.S.A.T. *Grant* in February 1941. Captain Long was a dental officer who served well during the battles of Bataan and behaved admirably at the POW camp at Cabanatuan. Like thousands of others, he had been a victim of starvation and disease while at Cabanatuan. I had been at his side in late 1942 when he received a letter announcing the death of his mother. He too was on the *Oryoku Maru* when it was bombed off shore at Olongapo Naval Yard. Like Jay Ryan, he was able to swim ashore. He was on the hellship *Enoura Maru* when it was bombed offshore at Formosa. During the bombing an overhead steel beam fell on Cyrus and pinned him down. He was then shot and killed by a Japanese marine. I myself had been aboard the *Enoura* in March of 1944 when it was under attack but was not hit.

Colonel William "Rhiney" Craig was another of my friends who went down some forks in a road not of choice. I had found early that Rhiney and I had both attended Lincoln Memorial University, a small college in Tennessee where we had had similar experiences. Chief of surgery at Sternberg and at General Hospital #2 in Bataan, he ranked me by two grades, but partly due to our similar background we became good friends. During our overnight stay at Camp #1 he had publicly paid me one of the highest compliments ever. He said that if he ever had a son he would name that child John.

Later at Cabanatuan he showed great courage in facing the Japanese, fighting hard for better food and medicine. He remained in the Philippines until December of 1944 when he, along with Ryan, Long, and hundreds of others, was crowded into the hold of the *Oryoku Maru*. When the ship was bombed, Colonel Craig was badly wounded. His dear friend Colonel William North swam ashore with Craig in tow. Colonel North dressed his wounds, and on December 23 Craig was put aboard the *Enoura Maru* at San Fernando enroute to Takoa, Formosa, where it was heavily bombed. Unlike Cyrus Long, "Rhiney" was one of the survivors. He was then transferred to the *Brazil Maru* where he lived until January 27, 1945. He died of wounds and starvation. His body was thrown overboard.

A fourth friend, spiritual guide, and barber while at Cabanatuan was Robert Preston Taylor (later Major General and Chief of Chaplains in the Air Corps). After the terrible hardships he endured on Bataan and at Cabanatuan he was to be subjected to almost unbelievable torture. After all these trials he was placed in the holds of the *Oryoku Maru*. When the *Oryoku Maru* was bombed and sunk, Taylor made his way out of the sinking ship and swam ashore. He was with Jay Ryan and the others held on the infamous tennis court for six days before being moved to San Fernando and herded aboard the ill-fated *Enoura Maru*. As the survivors were being placed in the forward hold of the freighter, Chaplain Taylor and Chaplain Dawson stood together waiting their turn to go into the hold. Chaplain Dawson, a dear friend of Taylor's, was signalled to enter the forward hold and Taylor was turned back and ordered to go into the after hold. Several days out, this doomed ship was bombed. The forward hold with Chaplain Dawson in it received a direct hit and all were killed. Taylor, the first to be directed to the after hold, was made aware of the vagaries of chance. Over 600 survivors were transferred to the *Brazil Maru*. Although the conditions on the *Brazil* were horrible and many like Rhiney Craig died of disease, starvation, and exposure, Taylor was one of 400 who survived until the ship arrived at Moji, Japan. After more hardships in Japan and Korea, he was released in September 1945. He had been through hell several times but was still alive.

At war's end Captain Jack Comstock was being held at Bilibid Prison, awaiting transport to Japan. He became a career army man.

I have many others in mind whom I knew well, but these are a few who exemplify the ultimate in human suffering and sacrifice.

CHAPTER 18

Home Again

On my way home across the Pacific I had the first symptom of tuberculosis. I was out on the deck with my fellow ex-POWs. It was a cool night and as I sat with my back against the rail, I developed a pleuritic pain in my right chest. This pain was gone in 48 hours and did not return until some weeks later. After we docked in San Francisco, all recovered military personnel were hospitalized at Letterman General Hospital for a physical survey. There my X-ray showed an infiltration in the right apex. The news was a stunning blow: I had gone through more than four years of hell and now this!

The subsequent story is one of sad miscalculations by me and the Army Medical Corps. Soon after I learned about my misfortune, I was shipped by train to Camp Butner, North Carolina. I spent two weeks at "Hotel" Butner, which was suited for little more than triage. The staff spent no great energy in confirming the diagnosis or in beginning treatment. Instead they decided that I was in the wrong place and that I should be returned by rail to Bruns General Hospital in Santa Fe, New Mexico, which they presumed to be a center for pulmonary disease. At Bruns I was put on a large open ward with about 60 other tuberculosis patients, had a chest X-ray, and was given three cardboard cups to spit in – one a day for three days. Outside of that flurry of activity, I was just a boarder for the three months that I was there.

A young lieutenant examined my chest with a stethoscope only one time and in a very perfunctory manner. The lieutenant made daily rounds, listened to complaints, and wrote orders for sleeping pills and laxatives. He was friendly, but it was obvious that he was interested only in getting out of the army and returning to a surgical residency. This was the image generally projected by the reserves. They had been involved in a war that separated them from family and delayed their professional life. I could not blame them for their desire to get military life behind them.

At Bruns an elderly colonel (regular army) was chief of medicine in the hospital. This gentlemen made rounds once a week. His movements through the ward were hurried, and as he progressed he slapped his stethoscope against his thigh as if it were a riding crop. At times, I felt that he was a cavalry man at heart. As he went from one bed to the next, he would ask, "How are you, young man?" Regardless of the answer he would reply, "That's fine, that's fine," and pass on to the next bed. Finally, three or four officers were cued to answer the colonel, "I feel awful." When he arrived next week he began the routine, "How are you, young fellow?" Each patient answered, "I feel miserable" or "I feel awful." The colonel never missed a stride or failed to slap his thigh with his stethoscope as he answered, "That's fine, that's fine." The accompanying nurse and young ward surgeon were perfect stoics; they had no reaction, and the imperturbable colonel moved on.

After two months at Bruns I received notice that I was to be moved. Someone, perhaps in Washington, decided that we should be moved to suitable facilities near our homes. The suitable facility nearest my home was at Swannanoa, North Carolina, and I traversed the continent for the third time. At Swannanoa, I went through the same routine as at Bruns, except there were more USO shows and more arts and crafts, and my mother, father, and girlfriend could visit me. The treatment was rest, rest, and more rest. I was at Swannanoa through the spring of 1946 when, as I really should have expected, another move was announced. Swannanoa was declared not suitable for processing officers with tuberculosis. Therefore, back across the continent I went to Fitzsimmons Hospital in Denver, Colorado. By then I felt that I was the most traveled patient in the armed service. The treatment was about the same as before, but the food was much better.

I tried to forget the six years that I had already lost out of my life. I read a lot, listened to the radio, and wanted to believe that I would remain there at Fitzsimmons until I was well, but in early September of 1946 I received another jolt. I was to appear before a board to determine whether I should receive a medical discharge. I was discharged on partial disability, but I was not advised about what to do after discharge. I was so sick of being shunted around that I made my destination home. I arrived there in September 1946, and it was a blessed relief to be at home with my parents. I began to feel better, and with that came hope that I might be able to resume my profession. I corresponded with the dean of the Medical College of Virginia, at Richmond, and requested a place on the resident staff in pediatrics. Dr. Lee Sutton, dean and professor of pediatrics, readily honored my request, and I reported for duty at MCV in December 1946.

After one day on the wards, I felt utterly weary, so that by the end of the day I could barely walk. This ordeal continued until the last week of December when I was suddenly made aware of the true state of things. I came to my room at the end of the day and started to undress when I suddenly began to cough and raised several tablespoonfuls of bright red blood. At that moment the prospects of a professional life seemed to fade completely away. There was nothing to do but notify Dean Sutton, who immediately put me in the university hospital. The staff there were very energetic in trying to determine the nature of my problem. A chest X-ray showed infiltration in the right upper lobe and a pneumonic consolidation in the right lower lobe. Several specimens of sputum were examined, and the young pulmonary specialist in charge of my case induced pneumothorax on the right; after a few more days I was transferred to McGuire General Hospital in Richmond, Virginia, where I was placed on the TB ward. I was despondent, but my good friend and former classmate, Dr. Dewitt

Daughtry, was on the surgical staff at McGuire, and he cheered me a great deal by his visits. And my future wife Evelyn came to see me.

The bedrest and pneumothorax were continued. The staff at McGuire took a great deal of interest in me, largely because none of them had ever seen a case of tuberculous pneumonia before. No one would show me my X-rays because (I was told later) they feared that if I saw the X-rays, I might give up.

When I arrived at McGuire, there was in progress a double-blind study of the use of streptomycin in the treatment of tuberculosis. The method of selecting those eligible for treatment was such that I drew a black ball and was unluckily bypassed. My treatment consisted of bedrest and continuation of the pneumothorax. I finally became afebrile, and my sputum became negative for acid-fast bacilli. After several months of sheer tedium I was weary of both the system and myself, and given my experience of being shunted around, I felt utterly frustrated. The staff, who seemed to understand what was going on, decided to send me home on leave in mid–May 1947.

I was very happy to be at home, but I should never have imposed myself on my elderly parents. Time, events, and frustration had clouded my judgment. My parents, however, never betrayed for one moment that my presence was an imposition. Of course, Evelyn and I exchanged letters and visits. I finally proposed marriage, and we were wed at Evelyn's home on August 30, 1947. The minister, a dear friend, related to his daughter after the wedding that he had never seen a sorrier looking prospect for a groom. He was right! I was haggard, as my photos attest, and woefully underweight.

After I left Richmond, my pneumothorax was continued at home by a physician friend, and, with the help of Chief of Staff Dr. Lonnie Hamilton, I arranged to work as a resident at the Pine Breeze Sanatorium in Chattanooga, Tennessee. My exhilaration was indescribable – I had a new bride and I was, after seven lost years, going to practice my profession. Before our arrival, Dr. Hamilton had an old abandoned operating room furnished for our quarters. Our bedroom, formerly the operating room, had green tile walls and a green tile floor that sloped, not very gradually, to a large drain in the center of the floor. At times we retired at night only to wake up the next morning to find that our bed had migrated to the center of the room. The dressing and shower rooms served as our kitchen, breakfast room, and bathroom. Imagine beginning married life with three showers, three commodes, and three sinks!

I only worked about four hours a day at Pine Breeze; truthfully, I was not able to do much more. Dr. Hamilton prescribed streptomycin for me in the dosage of 1 gram per day for 90 days. He showed Evelyn how to inject the drug in my gluteus maximus. Evelyn's forte is food science, not nursing; I had a sore rear for three months.

Evelyn and I remained content and happy until late April 1948 when Dr. Hamilton, who was continuing my pneumothorax, noted by fluoroscopy that there was fluid in the right pleural cavity. I was more easily fatigued and had a cough and a late afternoon fever. Dr. Hamilton ordered sputum exams, which turned out to be positive. I could not have been more depressed.

Eight years were gone from my life and now I seemed farther from my goal than ever before. Dr. Hamilton arranged for me to be admitted to the VA hospital in Oteen, North Carolina, where I was continued on bedrest and pneumothorax. In about four months, the fever and cough were gone, my appetite was good, and I had gained weight.

I even began to feel good enough to appreciate the ironic humor of the letter I received from the General Accounting Office in July 1948 – almost seven and a half years after the fact. I had been overpaid, it seems, in December 1940, when I reported three days later to Fort Knox. The U.S. government now wanted my certified check or money order for $12.31.

In November the doctors decided that I was a candidate for surgery. Dr. James Farnsworth, the ward surgeon who had become my friend as well as my doctor, presented my case to the surgical conference. Later that day he made a special trip back to the ward to let me know that the decision was made and that I was to have a right pneumonectomy in three days. He also related that Dr. Julian Moore of Asheville, North Carolina, had walked in at the end of the conference. Dr. Moore, the first well-trained thoracic surgeon to practice in North Carolina, had a surgical practice in Asheville, but served as a consultant to Oteen and did some surgery there. Dr. Moore walked up to the screen, looked at my X-ray and announced, "I will take that case." He did, and decided, after opening my chest, that the lung should not come out. He drained the pleural cavity and removed a markedly thickened pleura from my right lung. I made a good recovery from the surgery. My right lung completely re-expanded, and I began to hope.

By May 1949 my disease was quiescent, and I was allowed a few leaves of absences from the hospital to visit Evelyn, who was acting as housemother in the Assembly Inn at Montreat College. On one of those visits Evelyn became pregnant. She left her job at Montreat two months before the school year was out, and we lived from May 1 to July in a log cabin on her parents' farm. Then we moved to Black Mountain, where I served as staff physician in the TB sanatorium. Finally, afer nine years of waiting, I was treating patients. It took several years for me to regain my strength, get more training, and finally begin a private practice. In September 1956 I began my practice of internal medicine and cardiology in Greensboro where I was able to practice without interruption for 30 years. My only residuals are a scarred lung, a calcified pleura, chronic bronchitis, and a small area of bronchiectasis.

I suppose I could easily be critical, but instead I am thankful for the 30 years I was able to practice medicine in my chosen field. I was a victim, like so many others, of the tremendous turmoil and confusion that inevitably accompany a terrible war.

Appendix

Reproduced on these pages is the card presented to the author by his fellow prisoners at Kamiso. The prisoners had since been dispersed to Nisi-Asibetu and Bibai. The card was first signed at Nisi-Asibetu, then carried to Bibai and signed by the men from Kamiso who had been moved there.

CAPT. J. R. BUMGARNER

✚ MEDICAL CORPS ✚
UNITED STATES ARMY

You came to us at Kamuso when morale
was very low,
And the Nips were very trying - improvements
were so slow,
When men went to Cemento - scarce knowing
how they did it,
If we had'int been there to see it - we could
never have believed it.
When Death stood near the door - hunger and
starvation too,
You came with a helping hand - a bolt
from out the blue.

Although not of our country - you didn't
care a fig,
You went in with tenacity - with heart so
strong and big,
Your patience was outstanding - your treatment
deft and sure,
And when short of medicines - your humour
was a cure.
British troops will remember - this expression
please accept
We salute you as a gentleman, and never
will forget.

SIR,

ON THIS HAPPY DAY OF OUR RELEASE
WE, ALL THE UNDERSIGNED BRITISH
W.O. N.C.O's AND MEN WISH TO
EXPRESS TO YOU OUR PROFOUND
GRATITUDE AND THANKS FOR YOUR
ASSISTANCE IN HELPING US PULL
THROUGH THE TRYING ORDEAL OF OUR
BLACKER DAYS AS PRISONERS OF THE
JAPANESE AT KAMIISO CAMP.

WE WILL NEVER FORGET YOUR
ABILITY, TENACITY, PATIENCE AND
DISCRETION DURING THOSE DAYS
AND WISH YOU, WITH ALL OUR
HEARTS A LONG HAPPY AND
PROSPEROUS LIFE.

NISI- ASIBETU. JAPAN.
   AUGUST . 1945.

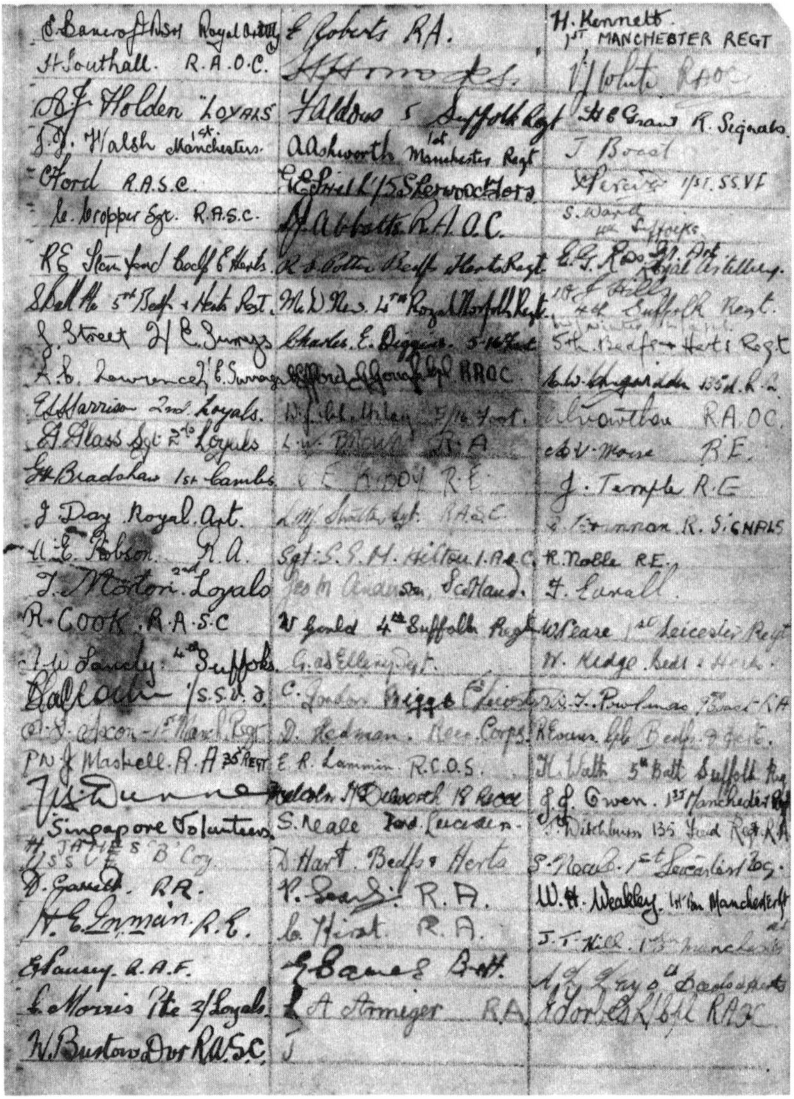

WE THE UNDERSIGNED FROM BIBAI
WISH TO ASSOCIATE OURSELVES WITH THE
SENTIMENTS EXPRESSED BY OUR COMRADES
DETACHED AT NISI-ASIBETSU.

Military History

John R. Bumgarner, M.D., was called to active duty as 1st Lt., 5th Medical Battalion, on December 7, 1940, at Fort Knox, Kentucky. After training at Fort Knox, December 9–20, 1940, and at Fort Custer, Michigan, December 20, 1940–January 1, 1941, he was ordered to the Philippine Islands. Bumgarner served as ward physician at Sternberg General Hospital, Manila, February 20–December 24, 1941. He was promoted to captain on December 24, 1941, and served as physician on a medical ward of General Hospital #2 from December 25 until April 9, 1942. From April 9, 1942, until September 2, 1945, Bumgarner was a Japanese prisoner of war. He was promoted to major on September 2, 1945. During the period November 2, 1945–May 8, 1949, he was a patient in several army and veterans hospitals, suffering from advanced pulmonary tuberculosis. Bumgarner received the Bronze Star for his service in Bataan.

Index